ANESTHETICS

Surgery Without Pain

These and other books are included in the
Encyclopedia of Discovery and Invention series:

ANESTHETICS
Surgery Without Pain

by JUDITH C. GALAS

The ENCYCLOPEDIA of
D·I·S·C·O·V·E·R·Y
and **INVENTION**

P.O. Box 289011, SAN DIEGO, CA 92198-9011

Library of Congress Cataloging-in-Publication Data

Galas, Judith C., 1946-
   Anesthetics: surgery without pain / Judith C. Galas.

      p. cm.—(The Encyclopedia of discovery and invention)
   Includes bibliographical references and index.
   Summary: Traces the history and development of
anesthesia, from the days before anesthetics were
discovered, to the modern age and a look at the future.
   ISBN 1-56006-224-X (alk. paper)
   1. Anesthesia—History—Juvenile literature.
[1. Anesthesia—History]   I. Title.   II. Series.
RD79.G35 1992
617.9'6—dc20   92-27852
                                                      CIP
                                                      AC

Contents

■■

Herbs, alcohol, and magic;
The discovery of ether;
Religious and medical obstacles;
Experiments with inhaling gases.

The discovery of anesthesia;
Pioneers in anesthesia research;
The first painless surgery;
The fight for fame and fortune.

Ether's reputation spreads;
The advent of chloroform;
Public acceptance of anesthesia;
Renewed interest in nitrous oxide;
New possibilities for surgery.

The power of cocaine;
Blocking the nerves;
Spinal blocks;
Infiltration anesthesia;
The search for better anesthetics.

Synthetic anesthetics;
Procaine and barbiturates;
Intravenous anesthesia;
Safer gases;
Endotracheal anesthesia.

Foreword

The belief in progress has been one of the dominant forces in Western Civilization from the Scientific Revolution of the seventeenth century to the present. Embodied in the idea of progress is the conviction that each generation will be better off than the one that preceded it. Eventually, all peoples will benefit from and share in this better world. R.R. Palmer, in his *History of the Modern World,* calls this belief in progress "a kind of nonreligious faith that the conditions of human life" will continually improve as time goes on.

For over a thousand years prior to the seventeenth century, science had progressed little. Inquiry was largely discouraged, and experimentation, almost nonexistent. As a result, science became regressive and discovery was ignored. Benjamin Farrington, a historian of science, characterized it this way: "Science had failed to become a real force in the life of society. Instead there had arisen a conception of science as a cycle of liberal studies for a privileged minority. Science ceased to be a means of transforming the conditions of life." In short, had this intellectual climate continued, humanity's future would have been little more than a clone of its past.

Fortunately, these circumstances were not destined to last. By the seventeenth and eighteenth centuries, Western society was undergoing radical and favorable changes. And the changes that occurred gave rise to the notion that progress was a real force urging civilization forward. Surpluses of consumer goods were replacing substandard living conditions in most of Western Europe. Rigid class systems were giving way to social mobility. In nations like France and the United States, the lofty principles of democracy and popular sovereignty were being painted in broad, gilded strokes over the fading canvases of monarchy and despotism.

But more significant than these social, economic, and political changes, the new age witnessed a rebirth of science. Centuries of scientific stagnation began crumbling before a spirit of scientific inquiry that spawned undreamed of technological advances. And it was the discoveries and inventions of scores of men and women that fueled these new technologies, dramatically increasing the ability of humankind to control nature—and, many believed, eventually to guide it.

It is a truism of science and technology that the results derived from observation and experimentation are not finalities. They are part of a process. Each discovery is but one piece in a continuum bridging past and present and heralding an extraordinary future. The heroic age of the Scientific Revolution was simply a start. It laid a foundation upon which succeeding generations of imaginative thinkers could build. It kindled the belief that progress is possible as long as there were gifted men and women who would respond to society's needs. When Antonie van Leeuwenhoek observed *Animalcules* (little animals) through his high-powered microscope in 1683, the discovery did not end there. Others followed who would call these "little animals" bacteria and, in time, recognize their role in the process of health and disease. Robert Koch, a German bacteriologist and winner of the Nobel Prize in Physiology and Medicine, was one of these men. Koch firmly established that bacteria are responsible for causing infectious diseases. He identified, among others, the causative organisms of anthrax and tuberculosis. Alexander Fleming, another Nobel Laureate, progressed still further in the quest to understand and control bacteria. In 1928, Fleming discovered penicillin, the antibiotic wonder drug. Penicillin, and the generations of antibiotics that succeeded it, have done more to prevent premature death than any other discovery in the history of humankind. And as civilization hastens toward the twenty-first century, most agree that the conquest of van Leeuwenhoek's "little animals" will continue.

The *Encyclopedia of Discovery and Invention* examines those discoveries and inventions that have had a sweeping impact on life and thought in the modern world. Each book explores the ideas that led to the invention or discovery, and, more importantly, how the world changed and continues to change because of it. The series also highlights the people behind the achievements—the unique men and women whose singular genius and rich imagination have altered the lives of everyone. Enhanced by photographs and clearly explained technical drawings, these books are comprehensive examinations of the building blocks of human progress.

ANESTHETICS

Surgery Without Pain

ANESTHETICS

Introduction

For thousands of years, people looked for a way to stop pain. They found temporary relief by eating herbs or drinking alcohol and stronger relief by taking narcotics such as opium. All of the early methods offered some pain relief for minor injuries and illnesses. But none of these remedies could protect a person from the intense pain that came during surgery.

Surgeons had to limit operations to those procedures that could be done quickly. Most patients could not survive intense pain for more than fifteen min-utes. But even short operations to amputate limbs, take babies from the womb, or remove tumors near the skin's surface caused great suffering. Some people preferred death to an operation.

On October 16, 1846, at Boston's Massachusetts General Hospital, the first painless surgery was performed before an audience of doctors. The patient was given ether, a gas that causes sleep when inhaled. From that moment on, pain was no longer a necessary part of surgery. With the first anesthetics, doctors found an important tool of modern surgery.

Ether, chloroform, and nitrous ox-

... TIMELINE: ANESTHETICS

1 > 2 > 3 > 4 > 5 > 6 > 7 > 8 > 9 > 10 >

1 ■ 1540
Valerius Cordus prepares ether.

2 ■ 1772
Joseph Priestley discovers nitrous oxide.

3 ■ 1800
Humphry Davy reports that nitrous oxide can dull pain.

4 ■ 1818
Michael Faraday mentions that ether kills pain.

5 ■ 1824
Henry Hickman uses carbon dioxide as an anesthetic on animals.

6 ■ 1831
Samuel Guthrie, Eugene Soubeiran, and Justus von Liebig independently discover chloroform.

7 ■ 1842
Crawford Long performs painless surgery using ether.

8 ■ 1844
Horace Wells uses nitrous oxide to stop pain during tooth extractions.

9 ■ 1846
William Morton administers ether while John Warren performs the first painless surgery before a group of doctors.

ide—the first anesthetics—entered the body through the lungs. No one knew how these drugs worked. Doctors soon realized, however, that the drugs that brought sleep and pain relief also could bring death. They knew they had much more to learn.

Since the late 1800s, doctors and researchers from around the world have met the challenge of learning about safer anesthetics and procedures. They have discovered a variety of anesthetics that have made surgery safer and less frightening for patients no matter their age or illness.

Discovering new ways to give these drugs also helped make anesthesia safer. Doctors learned that patients did not always have to breathe themselves into unconsciousness. Some pain-numbing drugs could be injected into the body while the patient stayed awake. Mothers watched without pain as doctors delivered their babies. Other patients stayed awake while surgeons operated on diseased or injured parts of the body.

Anesthesia researchers continue to search for better and safer ways to stop surgical pain. One day, their research may help them understand how to stop all pain, not just the pain that accompanies surgery and had for generations made people scream.

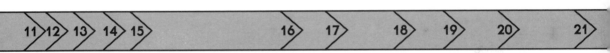

11 12 13 14 15   16 17 18 19 20 21

10 ■ 1847
James Simpson uses chloroform to relieve a patient's pain during childbirth.

11 ■ 1884
Carl Koller uses cocaine to numb the eye.

12 ■ 1885
Nerve-block anesthesia is introduced.

13 ■ 1892
Carl Schleich demonstrates infiltration anesthesia.

14 ■ 1898
August Bier uses spinal anesthesia on people.

15 ■ 1905
Alfred Einhorn introduces procaine, a synthetic anesthetic.

16 ■ 1934
Cyclopropane is used in surgery.

17 ■ 1942
Harold Griffith uses the muscle relaxant curare during surgery.

18 ■ 1956
Charles Suckling synthesizes halothane.

19 ■ 1965
Researchers synthesize isoflurane.

20 ■ 1975
Isoflurane is approved for use in U.S. hospitals.

21 ■ 1990
Sevoflurane, an improved fluorinated gas, is used in Japan.

The Unavoidable Agony

Ancient people lived with pain every day. They knew minor pain from headaches, cuts, and bruises. They also experienced the excruciating pain of severed limbs, incurable diseases, and surgery. Early people no more expected to control or eliminate pain than they expected to dim the sun. Pain was a powerful, uncontrollable force. They did, however, search for temporary pain relief.

Foraging for Plants

Early healers foraged in nature's plant pharmacy seeking analgesics, or painkillers. They also searched for anesthetics, which bring unconsciousness to a patient during illness or surgery. Mulberries, lettuce, leeks, dittany, and hellebore are plants that brought only minor pain relief. Plants like mandrake, marijuana, henbane, coca, and poppies contained stronger painkillers, or narcotics. The ancients also used alcohol to numb pain.

These healers did not understand how alcohol or the drugs from plants worked and therefore did not know how to control the drugs and their ill effects. As a result, their use sometimes led to death instead of relief.

Alcohol and narcotics cause some numbness or can make a person drowsy. They are not, however, safe or effective anesthetics. None can safely bring the total numbness necessary to keep a person unconscious but alive during surgery. Given these limitations, it is unlikely that early healers could have spared patients from the agony of a sharpened flint as it cut into muscle during surgery.

Yet surgeries were performed. Cave paintings dating back to 7000 B.C. depict amputations of arms and legs. A number of skulls unearthed in France have holes in them. Researchers date these skulls to 5000 B.C. and say the holes, known as trephinations, were made carefully by sharpened instru-

Before the advent of anesthesia, patients endured excruciating pain during surgery.

One particularly painful operation involved perforating the skull with surgical instruments. The resulting holes were called trephinations.

ments, probably during surgery.

No one knows for certain how prehistoric surgeons kept their patients from thrashing and screaming with pain during trephination. Signs of new bone growth around the holes indicate that Stone Age people endured the pain of head surgery and survived, although most patients probably were unconscious during the operation.

In South America, juice from the coca plant may have eased the pain from trephinations. Coca leaves contain cocaine, a pain-numbing substance. Some researchers think the surgeon chewed coca leaves and then spat the juice into the head wound while cutting through the patient's skull.

In China, perhaps as early as 3000 B.C., surgeons may have used acupuncture, a method of piercing the skin with thin needles and then rapidly twirling the needles. Acupuncture, the doctors

believed, channeled the body's natural energy along specific pathways to kill pain and restore overall health.

Acupuncture spread to Japan around 250 B.C. and to other parts of Asia. The hardship of traveling great distances and the differences in the religious beliefs and customs probably kept acupuncture from spreading to Europe and other faraway locations.

Spells and Potions

Whatever the operation, it is likely that surgeons throughout the world tried a combination of methods, spells, and potions to ease their patients' pain. Most likely, alcohol, one of the oldest pain relievers, flowed freely before surgery. Alcohol, even mixed with opium, as it often was, is not an effective anesthetic. It dulls a patient's senses but not enough to keep the person from feeling pain. But alcohol was readily available, easily made, and better than nothing.

Early people made alcoholic beverages by allowing fruits and grains to ferment. More sophisticated cultures learned how to distill liquors through a process of heating, evaporation, and condensation. This same process would eventually be used to create ether, one of the first truly reliable anesthetics.

Ether, however, is not mentioned in medical writings until the sixteenth century. Healers in the Middle Ages would try and fail with a great deal of magic and a number of potions before giving ether a serious look. For example, one thirteenth-century recipe for a four-day sleeping potion calls for equal amounts of tar and wax from a dog's ear. Some surgeons said patients would fall soundly asleep after eating soap or the fat from a man's liver or lizard oil.

The Sleeping Sponge

The sleeping sponge, also known as the surgical sponge, was probably the most widely used anesthetic in the Middle Ages. The sponge, saturated with a mixture of herbs and placed under the patient's nose, was supposed to render the patient unconscious. Theodoric, a monk and surgeon who lived in the thirteenth century, gave this recipe for making a sleeping sponge:

> Take of opium, of the juice of the unripe mulberry, of hyoscyamus, of the juice of the hemlock, of the juice of the leaves of mandragora, of the juice of the woody ivy, of the seeds of dock which has large round apples, and of the water hemlock each an ounce. Mix all of these in a brazen vessel, and then place it in a new sponge; let the whole boil as long as the sun lasts on the dog-days, until the sponge consumes it all. Place this sponge in hot water for an hour and let it be applied to the nostrils of him who is to be operated on until he has fallen asleep, and so let the surgery be performed.

Years later, a curious researcher followed the recipe and found that fumes from the sponge did not "make even a guinea pig nod." The sponge's special liquid, which contained juices from known narcotic plants, probably would have been more effective swallowed than sniffed from a sponge.

The surgical sponge did not bring the merciful sleep early surgeons were looking for, but they had the right idea.

While alcohol did not completely eliminate pain, it did relieve some of the agony of surgery. Here, a doctor tries to deaden a patient's pain with fumes from alcohol.

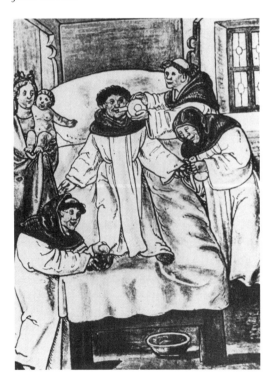

Inhaling sleep-inducing fumes eventually became the preferred method of applying anesthesia for surgery, but not for hundreds of years.

"Sweet Vitriol"

Suffering during surgery came close to ending in the sixteenth century when chemist Valerius Cordus and his contemporary Paracelsus, a noted Swiss physician, each worked with ether and studied its effects. About 1540, Cordus combined alcohol and the "sour oil of vitriol," or sulfuric acid, while working in his laboratory. He heated the mixture and collected the liquid that con-

The first picture ever made of an amputation, from a sixteenth-century book titled Field-Book of Wound Surgery.

About 1540, Valerius Cordus prepared a mixture of alcohol and the oil of vitriol, or sulfuric acid. The resulting liquid came to be known as "sweet vitriol."

densed from the steam.

The new mixture interested Paracelsus, who was among the first physicians to use chemicals as a way to cure illness. During one experiment, Paracelsus tested the liquid on chickens and wrote that it was associated with such a sweetness that

> it is taken even by chickens, and they fall asleep from it for a while, but awaken later without harm. . . . It quiets all suffering . . . relieves pain and quenches all fever, and prevents complications in all illnesses.

The liquid came to be known as "sweet vitriol" possibly because of the sweet sleep it caused.

Ether cannot do everything Paracelsus claimed it could. It will not cool a fever or prevent medical complications in all illnesses. He was, however, absolutely correct about one thing: it blocked pain.

Paracelsus died in 1541, but Cordus continued experimenting with sweet vitriol. Cordus was also interested in the treatment of diseases. He found that sweet vitriol helped dissolve other chemicals so they could be mixed into more effective medicines for lung diseases like pleurisy, whooping cough, and pneumonia. Cordus died only three years after Paracelsus and did not record any sleeping experiments with sweet vitriol. Sweet vitriol continued to be used as a treatment for asthma and other respiratory problems. In 1792, Wilhelmus Frobenius, a German apothecary, renamed it ether.

Almost three hundred years passed between the research of Cordus and Paracelsus and the use of ether to kill pain during surgery. For many reasons,

Although Paracelsus experimented with sweet vitriol, he was primarily interested in finding medical remedies to treat illness. He was not looking for an anesthetic.

people did not realize the value of the of the scientists' discovery.

First, Paracelsus and Cordus were not looking for an anesthetic. They were looking for better medications to treat illnesses. They were not seeking a way to bring unconsciousness during surgery and did not pursue that idea in their own research and experiments.

In addition, what little these scientists wrote about sweet vitriol was written in papers few doctors would ever read. These research papers were stored in libraries few could visit. Information about discoveries did not pass quickly from one scientist to another and to physicians.

Mysterious Methods

The discovery that inhaling ether caused a deep sleep also happened during a time when people feared witches and sorcery. They would have been suspicious of a liquid that mysteriously put people to sleep and of the physician who could quickly make a patient unconscious.

Also, most physicians were still hoping to use herbal mixtures to bring about sleep. Some people died from overdoses of common narcotics like opium, so physicians proceeded with caution. Surgeons could be jailed for misusing herbal potions or even accused of witchcraft and executed. Fear discouraged them from experimenting with untried methods like ether inhalation.

Religion also played a role in the Europeans' search for a substance to end pain. Many believed that God used pain to punish people for Adam and Eve's disobedience in the Garden of

In the late eighteenth century, Austrian physician Franz Anton Mesmer experimented with hypnotism—or mesmerism as it was called—to eliminate pain during medical procedures. Here, Mesmer treats a group of patients in a Paris salon.

Eden. Some wondered if they should interfere with God's plan.

The medical community, too, was an obstacle to the use of anesthesia. By the 1700s, doctors had grown in prestige and influence, and they did not want to be associated with old herbal remedies or questionable methods discovered in archaic laboratories.

Many prominent physicians were embracing newer methods of causing unconsciousness before surgery. Their methods, however, were not very effective. Men were beaten senseless. Women were made to faint. Surgeons used their fingers to squeeze arteries in the patient's neck. Shutting down these arteries stopped the blood flow to the brain and brought temporary unconsciousness. Stopping the blood flow, however, could also cause brain damage or death.

Physicians also tried more unusual methods to fight pain. They tightened clamps around an arm or leg before an amputation in the belief that compression would relieve pain. The clamps themselves, however, were excruciat-

ingly painful. Others applied snow to deaden feeling.

In the late 1700s, an Austrian physician named Franz Anton Mesmer, tried mesmerism, or hypnotism, with limited success. Mesmerism helped a person enter a trance during which a hypnotist told the patient he or she would feel no pain during a medical procedure.

The Speed of the Knife

Because hypnotism is based on a belief in the powers of the mind or spirit over the human body, hypnotism required the patient to believe that the mind could block out the body's pain. Faced with the surgical knife, however, many people were unable to believe that surgery would not hurt. Hypnotism was dropped as a method of preventing surgical pain, leading people to the conclusion that the surgeon's speed was always the best way to shorten pain. Intense pain could kill a patient by causing a heart attack. By necessity, operations lasted only about five to twenty

A patient writhes in agony as a surgeon cuts into his skull. A surgeon's speed with a knife was the best remedy for pain.

Swedish chemist Carl Wilhelm Scheele independently discovered the presence of oxygen, a colorless, tasteless, odorless gas. The bubbles in fermenting beer had attracted Priestley's scientific attention.

Laughing Gas

A year later, his experiments with oxygen led to his discovery of nitrous oxide, which would become the first gas successfully used to kill pain. Priestley's work with gases also revealed that patients could inhale medicines rather than swallow them.

Samuel Latham Mitchell, a physician and chemist in colonial America, took advantage of these discoveries by using these new gases in inhalation therapy with his patients. He experimented with nitrous oxide on animals to find ways to improve his treatments.

Swedish chemist Carl Wilhelm Scheele is one of two scientists who discovered the presence of oxygen in 1771.

minutes. Surgery was also limited to areas on or just under the skin. Typical operations were amputations of breasts and limbs, tumor removals, hernia repairs, tooth extractions, and plastic surgeries. No one could have survived the shock of deep, internal cutting.

The 1700s did not bring physicians or scientists closer to a successful use of anesthesia. But scientific experimentation flourished in the eighteenth century, and these experiments yielded knowledge that would prove essential to blotting out pain during surgery. Of particular importance was work done with various gases.

In 1771, Joseph Priestley, a British chemist and Unitarian minister, and

An eighteenth-century surgeon describes anatomy to a medical student. Increasing knowledge of anatomy and other aspects of medicine gradually led the way toward surgery without pain.

Because he nearly killed some animals during his research, Mitchell believed that nitrous oxide was a powerful poison capable of causing fevers, cancer, leprosy, and other diseases. His belief that nitrous oxide was deadly was based on opinion, however, not careful research

Mitchell sent his views on nitrous oxide and oxygen to British physician Thomas Beddoes, who had established the Pneumatic Institution for the treatment of diseases by inhalation. Beddoes gave the job of testing Mitchell's gas theories to his young assistant, Humphry Davy.

Mitchell's untested ideas had discouraged other chemists and physicians from breathing the gas. But Davy, who was bright and curious, decided to test nitrous oxide on himself. Instead of bringing illness or death, the gas made him feel happy, even giddy. He called the sweet-smelling gas "laughing gas"

and went on to test it on cats, dogs, birds, and rodents.

Davy loved the floating sensations he felt in his muscles and limbs when he inhaled nitrous oxide. He inhaled the

Samuel Latham Mitchell discouraged the use of nitrous oxide. He believed—incorrectly—that it was a deadly poison.

gas frequently and found it temporarily stopped the pain from headaches and toothaches. One night, Davy breathed in such a large amount of nitrous oxide that he passed out. He quickly came to and found his only side effect to be uncontrollable laughter.

In 1800, Davy wrote a book about his nitrous oxide experiments. Toward the end of the work, he wrote:

> As nitrous oxide in its extensive operation appears capable of destroying physical pain, it may probably be used with advantage during surgical operations in which no great [loss] of blood takes place.

Nitrous oxide's ability to destroy the sensation of pain intrigued Davy. He

Despite Mitchell's conclusions about nitrous oxide, the inquisitive Humphry Davy (top) decided to test the gas on himself. He found that it temporarily stopped pain and caused a pleasant floating sensation. An artist from Davy's time makes light of Davy's work in a cartoon depicting a lecture and demonstration on nitrous oxide.

might have devoted more time to his pain experiments had he not been given the honor of going to London's Royal Institution, where he devoted himself to other areas of science.

Enthusiasm for nitrous oxide among other researchers was waning. Physicians had become wary of a gas that could alter a patient's heartbeat and make the patient giddy without reason. Physicians who used the gas were denounced as quacks, and inhaling laughing gas became illegal in Great Britain.

Brilliant Ideas and Faulty Conclusions

Michael Faraday, Davy's student and laboratory assistant, conducted many gas experiments not only with nitrous oxide but also with ether. In 1818, in a small note in a scientific journal, he wrote that when ether is mixed with air and inhaled, it produces effects similar to those caused by nitrous oxide and that it could put people to sleep for hours. Faraday's casual reference to ether went unnoticed, and Faraday was too busy with other experiments to make people aware of ether's powers.

Henry Hill Hickman, a young British physician, had read articles on gases by Davy and Faraday. About twenty years after Davy gave up his work with nitrous oxide, Hickman was searching for a way to stop pain during surgery. He dreaded the shrieking and the terror-struck faces of the patients he was trying to help.

Hickman knew other physicians used some gases to treat diseases. He hypothesized that gases passing through the lungs and into the blood could cause a patient to fall into unconsciousness before surgery. Hickman discovered that when he gave small animals only carbon dioxide to breathe, they slipped into unconsciousness. Once asleep, the animals appeared to feel no pain when Hickman took snips of their ears and tails. Hickman's idea was brilliant. Many give him the credit for discovering that inhaling gas causes unconsciousness and blots out pain during surgery.

Unfortunately, Hickman chose to work with carbon dioxide. He chose carbon dioxide because he believed it would be the safest gas to inhale. He did not realize the animals fell asleep because the gas was suffocating them by taking the place of oxygen in their blood. He did not know the animals would have died if the operations had been long ones. He only knew that the gas made the animals fall asleep and

Michael Faraday recognized the powerful effects of inhaling ether in the early 1800s.

British physician Henry Hill Hickman rendered animals unconscious by giving them carbon dioxide to breathe. Hickman did not realize that this deprived them of oxygen and could suffocate them.

that while they slept, they did not feel surgical pain.

Hickman's experiments introduced the idea that gas inhalation could be an effective anesthetic during surgery. Convinced he had made a surgical breakthrough, he contacted England's Royal Society and its president, Sir Humphry Davy. Davy and the society ignored Hickman.

Davy had become a famous scientist. He had discovered several chemical elements and had invented a safety lamp for miners for which he would be warmly remembered. He paid little attention to his early work with gases.

Hickman died at the age of twenty-nine. Had Davy told him to try nitrous oxide instead of carbon dioxide, the doors to surgical anesthesia would have opened swiftly. As it was, the world was still nearly twenty-five years away from embracing anesthesia.

CHAPTER 2

Relief at Last

The gas experiments of Humphry Davy, Michael Faraday, and Henry Hickman brought little response from the medical community because most physicians could see little practical use for them. Some doctors did use oxygen, ether, and nitrous oxide to treat lung diseases like tuberculosis, but they had little success. The powerful effects of the gases, however, were frequently observed and felt, not in doctors' offices, but at parties and in traveling sideshows, where the gases had become a source of entertainment.

College students studying gases in their chemistry classes found that when they inhaled ether or nitrous oxide, they felt giddy. They indulged in these happy sensations at parties called "ether frolics," where the main event was inhaling sulfuric ether or nitrous oxide and then dancing, singing, and acting silly.

A Quiet Country Doctor

Dr. Crawford W. Long knew how to make ether and regularly gave ether parties at his home in the small village

Although the medical community did not yet recognize that ether and nitrous oxide could be used as anesthetics, the powerful effects of the gases did not go unnoticed. College students and others enjoyed the giddy, light-headed sensation they experienced when they inhaled the gases at "ether frolics."

of Jefferson, Georgia. Long noticed that many of his guests bumped into things when they danced around but that they never seemed to feel any pain. He often found bruises on his own body after an ether party but could not remember having hurt himself. These parties gave Long the idea that ether might be a useful anesthetic.

Long got a chance to test his ideas when James Venable came to his office complaining about two tumors on his neck. When Venable hesitated to have the tumors removed because he was afraid of the pain, Long suggested that Venable inhale ether. Ether had prevented Long from feeling his bruises,

Dr. Crawford W. Long (above) noticed that guests at his ether parties felt no pain when they injured themselves. Following these observations, Long performed the first surgery using ether as an anesthetic (below).

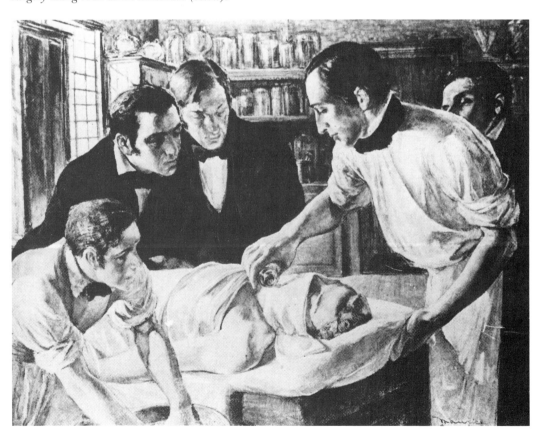

and he reasoned that maybe it would blot out his patient's pain during the operation.

On March 30, 1842, Venable held an ether-soaked towel to his face and quickly fell asleep. When he awoke, one tumor was gone; he had felt nothing. Venable paid Long two dollars for the operation and twenty-five cents for the ether.

Long had just performed the first surgery using ether, but instead of rushing to tell the world, he continued to live quietly as a country doctor.

Many people have wondered why Long did not tell his story until 1849, three years after others had shown that ether blocks surgical pain. Some historians think Long's medical practice started to decline when people heard he was experimenting with strange gases. Others believe Long simply did not realize the importance of what he had discovered. Because he lived far away from the big cities and medical schools, he may have been out of touch with the medical concerns of his time.

Whatever his reasons, Long did not announce his important discovery, and as a result, most people do not credit him with discovering surgical anesthesia. Great discoveries in science often happen through the work of many people, but the credit for the discovery usually goes to the person who attracts the most attention and who spreads the word about the discovery.

A Grand Exhibition

The honor of discovering surgical anesthesia, however, has never gone to just one person. Three Americans—dentists Horace Wells and William Thomas

Horace Wells pioneered the use of nitrous oxide as an anesthetic when, in 1844, he used the gas to eliminate the dreadful pain of pulling teeth.

Green Morton and physician Charles Thomas Jackson—fought hard for the honor. Each made an important contribution to the discovery of anesthesia.

In 1844, Horace Wells, a quiet, pleasant man of twenty-nine, had a small dental practice in Hartford, Connecticut. One December day, an advertisement in the *Hartford Courant* attracted his attention:

A GRAND EXHIBITION of the effects produced by inhaling NITROUS OXIDE, or LAUGHING GAS! will be given at UNION HALL THIS EVENING, Dec. 10, 1844. . . . FORTY GALLONS OF THE GAS will be prepared and [given] to all in the audience who desire to inhale it. . . . EIGHT STRONG MEN are engaged to occupy the front seats, to protect those under the influence of the Gas from injuring themselves or others. . . . THE EFFECT of the GAS is to make people who inhale it either Laugh, Sing, Dance, Speak or Fight. . . . Tickets 25 cents.

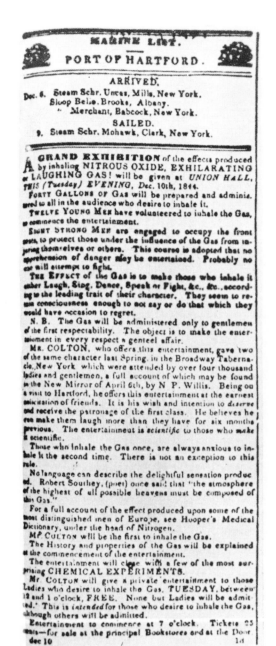

An advertisement in the Hartford Courant *attracted the attention of Wells and others who were interested in the effects of nitrous oxide.*

Wells and others from the town went to this public demonstration given by Professor Gardner Q. Colton. Colton was a showman, not really a professor. He made his living by giving talks about laughing gas and then letting someone from the audience inhale the gas and entertain the crowd with silly words and movements.

Wells and Samuel A. Cooley, a Hartford pharmacy clerk, stood up when Colton asked for volunteers. Wells inhaled nitrous oxide and felt a wonderful floating feeling, but he did not say or do anything particularly amusing. Cooley, however, began to run wildly around the stage and at one point banged his shins against a bench. Wells noticed that Cooley paid no attention to his injury. When Wells asked him about his leg, Cooley was surprised to see it was bleeding. He had not felt a thing.

Pulling Teeth

Wells had been looking for a way to eliminate the pain of pulling teeth, and he wondered if nitrous oxide might be the key to painless dentistry. He asked Colton to bring some of the gas to his office the next day.

On December 11, 1844, Wells inhaled the gas while his partner, John M. Riggs, pulled out one of Wells's wisdom teeth. Wells said he felt nothing more than a pin prick. He thought using nitrous oxide to kill pain was a wonderful idea, so he learned how to make the gas and gave it to several patients.

Usually, the gas worked, and his patients felt no pain. Sometimes, however, the gas did not stop the pain because Wells did not know exactly how much to give each patient. In spite of some failures, Wells was convinced that nitrous oxide could be used successfully, and he was determined to prove it.

In January, Wells traveled to Boston

to meet with a former dental student named William Morton. Morton thought Wells's idea had merit and suggested they discuss it with Charles Jackson, a respected chemist. Jackson completely rejected the idea. Nitrous oxide, he said, was dangerous, even deadly. Furthermore, it was not possible to have surgery without pain, he said.

Wells was not discouraged, however. While in Boston, he asked for and received permission to demonstrate the use of nitrous oxide at Massachusetts General Hospital. The hospital was the home of the famous surgeon and anatomy professor John Collins Warren, who was also dean of the Harvard Medical School.

Wells came to Warren's class carrying an airtight bag of nitrous oxide. He gave the gas to a Harvard student who had volunteered to have a tooth pulled after inhaling the gas. When Wells thought the student was asleep, he reached in and yanked out the tooth. Some accounts say the student yelled in

Wells demonstrated the use of nitrous oxide to the famous surgeon and anatomy professor John Collins Warren, dean of the Harvard Medical School.

pain; others say he simply moaned. The student insisted he had felt no pain. But the audience had heard him make noise, and they called Wells a fraud.

Doctors now know that patients can

Medical students carry on an animated debate over whether Wells successfully anesthetized a Harvard student before pulling his tooth.

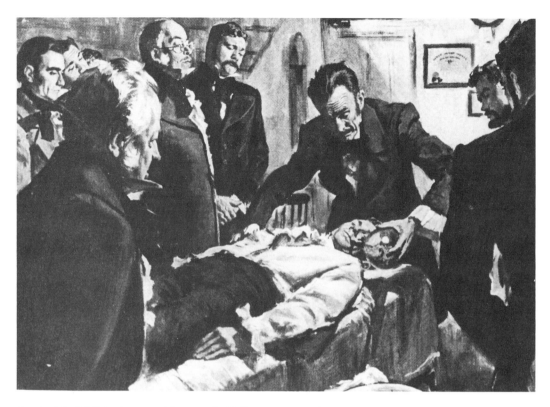

Inspired by Wells's nitrous oxide research, William Morton (below) speculated that ether might be used as an effective anesthetic. An audience watches eagerly as Morton administers ether to a patient (above).

groan while anesthetized, even though they do not feel pain. Some people speculate that Wells may have taken the gas away from the young man too soon or that the student may have been over-weight or a heavy drinker—two condi-tions that work against the gas's effects. Wells went home and continued his ex-periments, but ill health, possibly ner-vous exhaustion, forced him to leave his dental practice and his research.

Morton had seen Wells fail in Boston, but he still believed the use of a painkilling gas could increase business in his own dental practice. He went again to the chemist Jackson for some nitrous oxide. Jackson did not have any, but he suggested sulfuric ether instead. Jackson told Morton that ether was safe and that a person would fall asleep after sniffing ether fumes from a saturated cloth.

On September 30, 1846, Morton gave ether to Eben Frost and painlessly extracted one of Frost's teeth. Morton now fully believed Wells had been right. Surgery without pain was possible.

Morton decided that using ether during a full operation, not a simple tooth extraction, would prove to everyone he had discovered something truly important. He visited Warren and told him about his painless procedure but did not tell the surgeon he had used ether to kill the pain. Instead, Morton called his invention "letheon." Warren was definitely interested in anything that could stop pain.

An experienced surgeon, Warren had endured countless sessions of shrieking and pleading from patients during surgery. Surgeries were so painful that only three a month were performed at Massachusetts General.

Warren knew many people preferred to die rather than be saved through surgical torture. So, he agreed to let Morton try his new method on the next suitable patient.

"This Is No Humbug"

That patient was Gilbert Abbott, a twenty-year-old man with a rapidly growing neck tumor. Warren set the surgery for ten o'clock on Friday, October 16, 1846, and sent a letter to Morton inviting him to be present. Morton immediately took the plans for his ether inhaler to an instrument maker.

On the morning of the operation, Morton rushed to the instrument maker's shop. Nervous and impatient, he hurried the instrument maker along. Finally, fearing he would be late for his appointment, Morton grabbed the inhaler and dashed for the hospital.

Warren, believing Morton would

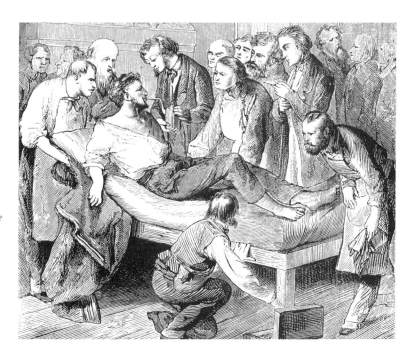

Morton made painless surgery a reality when he used ether to produce a deep sleep in surgical patient Gilbert Abbott. After this revolutionary demonstration, observer John Warren declared, "Gentlemen, this is no humbug."

The original Morton inhaler used in the historic surgery on Gilbert Abbott. With this inhaler, patients inhaled ether vapor through a wooden mouthpiece. The vapor brought welcome relief in the form of deep sleep.

not show, was about to cut into Abbott's tumor when Morton rushed into the operating room. He carried a large, glass globe with a wooden mouthpiece at one end and an open air hole at the other. A sea sponge in a puddle of colorless liquid was at the bottom.

Many stories say Warren turned to Morton with great annoyance and said, "Sir, your patient is ready." Morton gave the inhaler's mouthpiece to Abbott and told him to breathe deeply and regularly. As Abbott inhaled the air that traveled over the ether-soaked sponge, he fell into a deep sleep. Morton turned to Warren and said, "Dr. Warren, your patient is ready."

Warren made the first incision, but Abbott did not cry out. Warren cut deeper, but Abbott did not fight and plead for Warren to stop, as all the others had. Accustomed to operating quickly, Warren removed the tumor in less than three minutes. Abbott never stirred. When Abbott regained consciousness a few moments later, Warren asked him if he had felt anything. Only a scratching on his neck, he said. Warren turned to the audience and said, "Gentlemen, this is no humbug." Many reports say there were tears of relief in the famous surgeon's eyes. He had performed his first silent surgery.

Painless Amputation

Within days, two more operations were performed using ether. Like Abbott's operation, these surgeries were performed on the surface of the skin. Doctors wondered how ether would work during major surgery. They found out on November 1, when George Hayward amputated the leg of Alice Mohan, described as a delicate woman of twenty-one. Her leg was probably infected with tuberculosis, then a common disease affecting the bones and joints.

The young woman slept peacefully through the brief surgery, awakening only when Warren pulled on her sleeve and called her name. She opened her eyes, unaware that her leg had already been cut off. Warren held up her leg for her to see, and the audience broke into loud applause.

Shortly after these ether demonstrations, doctors tried to explain what had happened to the patients to make them fall asleep. They speculated that ether

Like Morton and Wells, Charles Jackson wanted to claim the sole honor of discovering anesthesia. Most historians credit the contributions of all three.

had caused changes in the blood supply to the brain. But no one had any evidence to support this idea, so it was soon abandoned.

People quickly began to wonder what they should call this new method of killing pain. Oliver Wendell Holmes, a well-respected physician and writer, suggested the word *anaesthesia*, which was based on the Greek word meaning "without feeling." Later, the second *a* was dropped in the spelling.

Not everyone was immediately excited about anesthesia. William H. Atkinson, a dentist, exclaimed:

> I think anesthesia is of the devil, and I cannot give my sanction to any Satanic influence which deprives a man of the capacity to recognize the law! I wish there were no such thing as anesthesia! I do not think men should be prevented from passing through what God intended them to endure.

Fame, Fortune, and Failure

Most people welcomed the discovery. They knew anesthesia would change medicine for the better. Anesthesia also changed the lives of the men who wanted to claim the honor of discovering it.

Horace Wells felt frustration. France had declared him the discoverer of anesthesia, but in his own country, Morton and Jackson were fighting for the honor. In 1848, exhausted, depressed, and possibly mentally ill, Wells drank chloroform and committed suicide by cutting open a vein.

William Morton always believed money and fame would come to the discoverer of painless surgery. Right after he pulled Frost's tooth, he rushed to patent his technique for using ether. At first, he refused to tell the surgeons at Massachusetts General what his powerful liquid really was. He thought if he disguised its appearance and odor and changed its name, doctors would think they could use this new discovery only after paying him.

The deception did not work. Doctors refused to use something they could not identify, and they refused to buy the rights to a scientific discovery they believed belonged to the world. Once Morton knew he would not gain great wealth, he fixed his attention on great fame.

Charles Jackson, who was never interested in the money, bitterly fought Morton for the fame. Each man wasted his energy, time, and money on the battle. Anger, exhaustion, and the weight of debts he could not pay drove Morton to a complete breakdown. He died penniless in a New York hospital in 1868.

Jackson, obsessed with claiming the sole honor of discoverer, went insane. He spent the last seven years of his life in an asylum and died in 1880.

Crawford Long, the little-known country doctor from Georgia, had returned to his medical practice after the Civil War. He had neither fame nor money and did not expect either to come his way. On June 16, 1878, he eased a woman's labor pains by giving her ether before he delivered her baby. He had a stroke and died in her home two hours later.

Today, no one is singled out as the discoverer of anesthesia. Some think the credit should go to Morton because he did the most to bring anesthesia to the attention of the medical community. Because Henry Hickman was the first to consider gas as a surgical anesthetic, some people think the credit really should go to him

In their lifetime, Wells, Morton, and Jackson each received credit and awards for their work. All of them, including Long and Hickman, have individual monuments that recognize their valuable contributions to the field of anesthesiology. Everyone agrees that together they gave the world the magic sleep that revolutionized medicine.

The Screams End Around the World

"I have seen something that will go around the world," said Dr. Henry J. Bigelow after the amputation of Alice Mohan's leg. He was right. The news of painless surgery spread quickly in the United States and in Europe. Within a year of Morton's demonstration, most doctors in the modern world used ether when they could.

Bigelow's father, physician Jacob Bigelow, wrote to a British friend and physician named Francis Boott and said that ether "promises to be one of the important discoveries of the present age." Jacob Bigelow described how he had taken his own daughter to Dr. Morton to have a tooth pulled. While under the effects of ether, she felt no pain.

Soon after he received Bigelow's letter, Boott's niece had a tooth pulled in

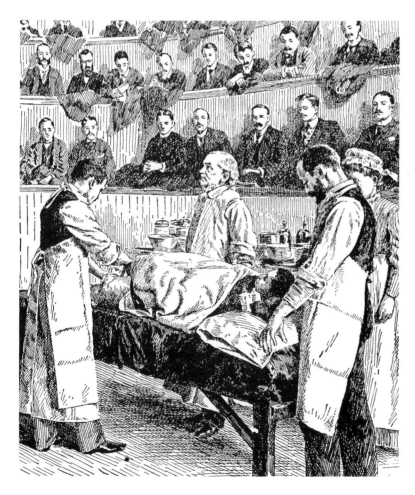

Word of Morton's success with ether spread quickly. Doctors welcomed the news that they could perform surgery without causing their patients grave pain.

his house. It was the first tooth extraction done using ether in Europe, and Boott quickly sent word to England's most famous surgeon, Robert Liston.

Like the American surgeon John Warren, Liston was all too familiar with the shrieks and pleadings he heard during surgery. He decided to try ether immediately.

Convincing Evidence

Liston was considered the quickest and most competent surgeon of his day. It was said that if a spectator sneezed, winked, or turned his head, he would miss the operation entirely. If ether worked for Liston, it would be assured a respected place in the operating rooms of Europe.

On December 21, 1846, at the University College Hospital of London, only two months after Morton's demonstration, Liston prepared to operate on a man's diseased thigh. The surgeon had done countless amputations, but this one on Frederick Churchill would be done with ether.

Liston had a reputation for being not only fast but also abrupt and rough-mannered. This day, however, he waited quietly until the ether put Churchill to sleep. Liston lifted the saw and cut through the thigh muscle. Churchill felt nothing. For the first time during surgery, Liston was not loud or brash. He gratefully declared the operation a success.

James Simpson, a popular, young Scottish doctor, heard about Liston's painless operation. Considered the most modern gynecologist in Europe, Simpson had been looking for something to relieve childbirth pain. When he tried ether in January 1847, Simpson was the first doctor to use it as an anesthetic during childbirth. Although the ether put the women to sleep, Simpson thought the vapors had too many problems.

Ether had a "disagreeable and very persistent smell," he said. His patients complained of throat irritation after inhaling the harsh vapors. Simpson also noticed that ether made his patients salivate too much, and often, it made them nauseous. Heavy salivation and vomiting increased the chance of foreign matter entering the lungs and causing pneumonia or suffocation.

Simpson was searching for a replacement anesthetic when Scottish chemist David Waldie told him about chloroform, a clear liquid that readily

The sweet-smelling chloroform vapors made painless childbirth possible.

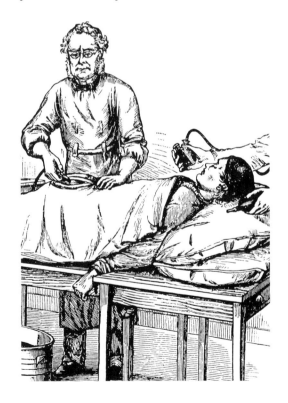

gives off vapors that cause unconsciousness. Chloroform had been discovered simultaneously and independently in 1831 by three chemists: Samuel Guthrie in the United States, Justus von Liebig in Germany, and Eugene Soubeiran in France.

Made in a laboratory, chloroform was a chemical curiosity made for no specific purpose. Waldie was one of only a few people who knew anything about it. Until Simpson, no one considered it as a possible anesthetic.

Painless Labor

Simpson experimented with chloroform on himself and two friends. The men gathered around a dining room table and took turns breathing the sweet-smelling vapors from the glasses of chloroform on the table. Suddenly, they fell asleep. When he awoke, Simpson decided chloroform was a promising anesthetic.

On November 5, 1847, Simpson successfully used chloroform on a woman during childbirth. The woman had already experienced a painful, three-day labor with another child. So after only a few hours of labor with this baby, she was happy to fall asleep with chloroform. Less than thirty minutes after she had inhaled the vapors, the baby was born. When the mother awoke, she thought she had taken a short nap and was astonished when her new baby was put into her arms. The baby was named Anesthesia.

Within ten days, Simpson had used the chloroform vapors in a variety of operations and had published his results. Chloroform, he wrote, had many advantages over ether. It was pleasant to

Dr. James Simpson of Scotland used chloroform to ease a woman's pain during childbirth in 1847. In honor of the painless birth, the woman named her baby Anesthesia.

inhale; it left no lingering, disagreeable odor; it worked more rapidly than ether; it probably was cheaper to use because less was needed; and it required no special inhaler.

Sin and Sorrow

Simpson was delighted, but many people within the religious and the medical communities were not. Their objections to painless childbirth had nothing to do with medicine, however. They believed that avoiding the pain of childbirth was a sin.

In 1591, a Scottish woman named Eufame Macalyne was burned at the stake in Edinburgh for trying to find a way to stop her childbirth pains. Her

Many people believed that alleviating the pain of childbirth was sinful. Simpson retorted that God used anesthetics by causing Adam to fall asleep before removing a rib to make Eve. This woodcut shows Adam fast asleep during Eve's creation.

crime had been ignoring God's command to Eve in the Garden of Eden: "In sorrow shall you bring forth children."

Almost three hundred years later, Simpson was making it possible for all women to escape childbirth pain. His colleagues were furious, but Simpson used the Bible to fight back. He told these men he did not believe God was so unforgiving. In fact, Simpson said, God had been the first to use anesthetics by causing Adam to fall asleep before he took out one of his ribs to make Eve.

The battle raged for six years and only stopped in 1853 when Queen Victoria, the recognized head of the Church of England, took chloroform during the birth of her seventh child, Prince Leopold. By the time she used it

again in 1857 during the birth of her eighth child, Princess Beatrice, the use of chloroform during childbirth was already accepted. Concerns about its safety, however, had grown.

Dangerous Vapors

Deaths from chloroform anesthesia were reported soon after Simpson's glowing announcements in 1847. By 1856, chloroform was directly linked to fifty deaths, a significant number considering that surgeries were still uncommon. Many of these deaths occurred during minor surgeries that were not done to save a patient's life.

At first, doctors did not know why

some people died from inhaling the vapors. They did not know how chloroform acted inside the body. As a way to protect their patients, doctors looked for outward signs to tell them when the gases were taking effect. They watched a patient's eyes and the rise and fall of the chest, observed the color of the skin, felt the pulse and the body's temperature, and watched the body struggle or jerk. If any of these signs signaled trouble, the gas was taken away and the doctor tried to revive the patient.

Physicians who closely watched a patient's heart rate soon learned that chloroform slowed the heart and sometimes caused it to stop beating altogether. By the late 1800s, autopsies would show that chloroform also damaged the liver.

For many physicians, however, chloroform's benefits outweighed its disadvantages. Because it was more pleasant to inhale, chloroform was used at more childbirths. Because the women were more relaxed during labor, chloroform reduced the number of hours of labor. As a result, fewer women died from the trauma of giving birth.

Easing a Soldier's Pain

Chloroform, when it was available, also eased the pain of thousands of injured soldiers in two wars—the American

Objections to the use of anesthesia during childbirth ceased when Queen Victoria used chloroform during the birth of her seventh child.

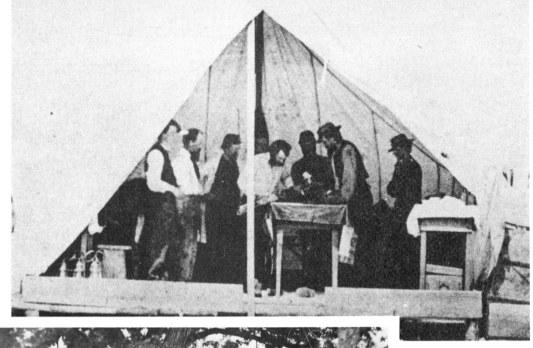

The American Civil War between the North and South was a bloody affair, with thousands of casualties (left). Surgeons in a federal hospital tent (top) operate on the leg of a fallen soldier. The man behind the operating table holds a chloroform-soaked rag over the patient's face.

Civil War in the 1860s and the Franco-Prussian War in 1870. Powerful, easy to give, and neither flammable nor explosive, chloroform remained a widely used anesthetic until safer inhalation anesthetics were discovered in the 1900s.

Its widespread use, however, did not keep physicians from trying to find ways to eliminate chloroform's dangers. The British, starting with Simpson, are credited with most of the early anesthesia experiments. They improved inhalers

for breathing chloroform and later ether and conducted education efforts about using anesthetics safely.

Searching for a Substitute

British physician John Snow, who had administered chloroform to the queen, was responsible for a great deal of the anesthesia research before his death in 1858. Within months of ether's use during surgery, Snow became inter-

JOHN SNOW'S CHLOROFORM INHALER

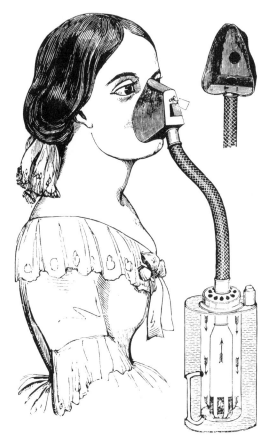

Dr. John Snow's chloroform inhaler, invented about 1850, allowed better control over the amount of anesthetic given to a patient. One important feature of Snow's inhaler is the valve attached to the patient's face mask. The valve can be opened or closed to control the amount of air mixing with the chloroform and thus control its strength.

Snow's inhaler has two metal cylinders, one inside the other. The smaller, internal cylinder, or evaporating chamber, contains liquid chloroform and a wire frame wrapped in absorbent paper. Cold water in the space between the two cylinders keeps the chloroform at an even temperature so that vapors do not build or evaporate too quickly.

When a patient inhales, fresh air is sucked into the outer cylinder through holes at the top. The air travels to the cylinder bottom where it enters the inner chamber. As the air rises, it passes over the chloroform-soaked paper picking up vapors. The vapors are carried out of the cylinder and up the breathing tube to the patient. Within minutes, the patient is unconscious and ready for surgery.

ested in the anesthetic and quickly learned how to give it to patients. Liston and other surgeons employed Snow as their anesthesiologist during surgery, which gave Snow many chances to observe the effects of anesthetics.

Snow made detailed studies of the effects of ether, chloroform, and other anesthetics, always testing the gases on himself first. He measured dosages and compared their effectiveness against the weight and the amount of blood in his experimental animals, usually rats and mice. He could accurately predict how much anesthetic it would take to make a person unconscious. He learned, for example, that twelve drops of chloroform would do the same work as four teaspoons of ether.

It was Snow who warned that chloroform, unlike ether, affected the heart. "I believe," he wrote, "that ether is incapable of causing sudden paralysis of the heart, which has happened during the administration of chloroform."

Snow unsuccessfully searched for an

anesthetic that would have chloroform's benefits without its dangerous side effects. When none was found, he helped to make anesthesia safer by identifying the four stages patients went through as they lapsed into full unconsciousness. Snow's descriptions of the states of relaxation, confusion, dreams, surgical anesthesia, and overdose or death guided physicians for another seventy years.

During the first stage, Snow said, patients were relaxed but awake and able to direct their movements. By the second stage, they felt and acted confused. In the third stage, they could not move voluntarily, even though their muscles might jerk and twitch. By the fourth stage, patients were fully unconscious, their only movement was the steady rise and fall of the chest. Snow reached a fifth stage in his experiments with animals, when their breathing stopped altogether.

Improving Inhalers

In addition to this research, Snow also made important contributions to anesthesiology by making improvements to inhalers. He designed a flexible, snug mask that closely resembles today's face masks. His ether inhalers had enlarged breathing tubes and coils that made the air circulate over the ether several times so the air the patient breathed would be saturated with ether. Water in the inhalers warmed the ether, which made the liquid give off more vapor.

Snow also devised better chloroform inhalers after he decided the anesthetic was more versatile than ether. The inhalers were smaller and easier to carry than the ether inhalers. Just like

the ether inhalers, the chloroform inhalers regulated the temperature of the anesthetic liquid so the anesthesiologist could better control the amount of vapor the patient inhaled.

Snow's knowledge of anesthetics and their effects was unmatched by anyone at that time. His careful research and observations, his inhalers, and his concern for patients' safety brought respect to the study of anesthetics and to the profession of anesthesiology. Because of his many contributions, Snow is considered the first anesthesiologist.

European physicians like Snow did much to make chloroform the most widely used anesthetic in Europe. Ether, which caused fewer problems in the op-

British physician John Snow is considered the first anesthesiologist because of his many contributions to anesthesia research.

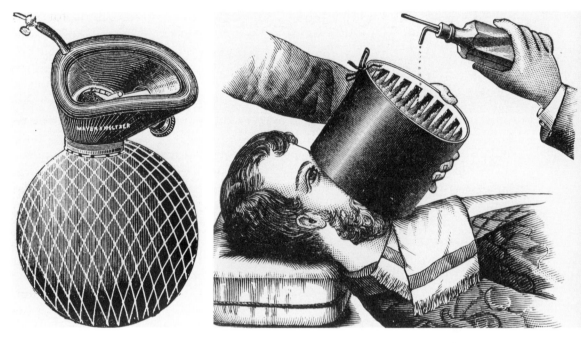

Nineteenth-century doctors and inventors improved anesthetic inhalers. The two inhalers (above) work by giving the patient ether-saturated air to breathe which brings on deep sleep. These and other inhalers gave anesthetists more control over the amount of vapor patients inhaled than did the old-fashioned ether-soaked rag.

erating room, was used more widely in the United States where hospitals were smaller and not as well equipped. Concern about both gases, however, and the continuing search for a truly safe anesthetic prompted European and American doctors to take a second look at nitrous oxide.

Rekindling Interest in Nitrous Oxide

Nitrous oxide had been abandoned after Horace Wells's unsuccessful attempt to prove it was an effective anesthetic. Gardner Colton, the sideshow professor who first introduced the sweet-smelling gas to Wells, rekindled its popularity in the late 1860s.

Colton had continued to demonstrate nitrous oxide and knew it quickly brought unconsciousness. He opened the Colton Dental Association in New York, and after twenty-three days, the office staff had pulled almost three thousand teeth. Nitrous oxide had ushered in painless dentistry.

Colton started dental offices in several eastern cities. One of his ads in 1869 read, "31 1/2 Miles Long." He estimated that if everyone who had used nitrous oxide stood in a line, the line would be 31 1/2 miles long.

In addition to spreading the word about painless tooth extraction, Colton also improved the bags that held the gas and increased the amount of gas patients inhaled. He sailed to Europe and spread the news about nitrous oxide to European dentists. All of this activity made it possible for Colton to do what

Wells could not—interest physicians in trying nitrous oxide as a safe, surgical anesthetic.

An Ideal Anesthetic?

Nitrous oxide seemed to be an ideal anesthetic. It did not cause vomiting. Unlike chloroform, it was not thought to be toxic or to have a significant effect on the breathing or heart rate. It was not known to affect the liver and kidneys. Unlike ether, it was not flammable. Its biggest drawback was that it could not produce the deep or lasting unconsciousness necessary for major surgery.

Edmund Andrews, a Chicago physician and researcher, combined nitrous oxide with oxygen and found that the combination prolonged the anesthetic effects of nitrous oxide. In 1868, he performed the first major surgery with nitrous oxide.

The gas, however, still could not produce the deep anesthesia chloroform and ether made possible. Nitrous oxide was also difficult to carry from place to place. Many surgeons operated in their patients' homes. Ether and chloroform were liquids that could be carried in a jar, but nitrous oxide was a gas that had to be carried in immense airtight bags or later in pressurized tanks.

The benefits of nitrous oxide were not fully appreciated until the 1930s when anesthesiologists learned to combine anesthetics to improve their effectiveness.

The Gift of Time

In the mid-1800s, anesthetics changed surgery from a battle using strength and speed to a fight for life using knowledge and skill. These gases gave surgeons the gift of time. With their patients asleep, surgeons now had time to repair injured or diseased body parts rather than just quickly cut them off.

Because it is a gas, nitrous oxide was difficult to transport. Surgeons had to use airtight bags or pressurized tanks to carry it from place to place.

Surgeons still worked quickly, however. For the first few years, patients inhaled anesthetics in a hit-and-miss fashion from saturated rags or from crude inhalers. Anesthesiology was a primitive science, and the first anesthesiologists knew almost nothing about how much anesthetic would be safe or effective. Most patients remained unconscious for only two or three minutes. The pain was gone, but the need for speed was not.

More and better anesthetics and more ways of using them made better surgery possible, but other surgical improvements were also happening. A growing awareness of germs and a desire to keep wounds clean meant that anesthesia could be used more successfully.

In his pioneering studies, French chemist Louis Pasteur demonstrated that germs cause infection and disease.

Pasteur's discoveries prompted surgeon Joseph Lister to use carbolic acid to kill germs during surgery.

Possibilities Unfold

When French chemist Louis Pasteur showed in the 1860s that unseen germs caused infection, surgeon Joseph Lister began a campaign to kill germs during operations. He soaked surgical instruments in germ-killing carbolic acid, he sprayed the acid around the operating room, and he put antiseptic, or germ-free, bandages on incisions. Infection rates dropped dramatically, and so did the death rate from surgery. Together, germ-free surgery and the painkilling powers of anesthetics made surgical progress possible.

For surgery to progress even further, surgeons needed safer anesthetics that were also easier to use. The known

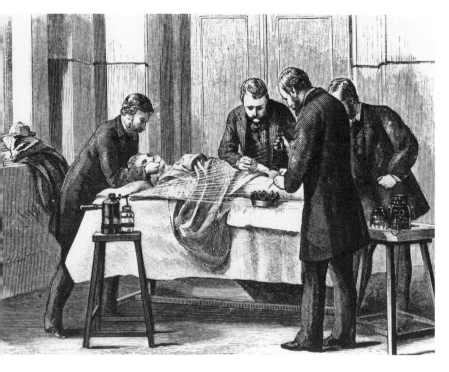

A nineteenth-century engraving depicts the use of antiseptic spray to kill deadly germs in an operating room. Germ-free surgery greatly advanced the science of medicine as did safer and more effective anesthetics.

gases were better than anything doctors could have imagined, but they had drawbacks.

Chloroform put a great strain on the body's heart and other organs, so it was not safe for patients who were already too old or too weak from sickness. Ether, with its harsh, irritating vapors, was not easily taken by children or nervous, excitable adults who fought the ether mask. Nitrous oxide was hard to transport and did not bring deep anesthesia.

Surgeons also needed an anesthetic for small, simple operations. Patients who needed minor surgery often had to endure painful cuts without anesthetics. Because ether and chloroform could be dangerous, they were saved for operations where the need to save the patient's life offset the risks of inhaling a gas.

Surgeons also needed anesthetics

that could be used for eye and head surgeries. The gases all required face masks, which got in the way during operations on the eyes, mouth, or face. Also, doctors could not perform eye surgeries on patients who were unconscious from a general anesthetic. These patients could not hear, so they could not follow directions to keep their eye still and open or to tilt their head in a certain way.

By the 1870s, surgeons were looking for anesthetics that patients did not have to breathe and that could numb the pain only in the part of the body that needed to be cut. They also wanted anesthetics that were less stressful to the body. During the late 1800s, the drug cocaine and a method of applying local anesthesia came together to meet these more specific needs.

Local Anesthesia

The idea of stopping pain by numbing the surface of the body was familiar to nineteenth-century researchers. People knew that intense cold could dull or stop pain. In the 1600s, surgeons rubbed or held snow against the flesh so they could painlessly cut on the skin's surface. Surgeons who amputated the legs of Napoleon's soldiers during their winter retreat from Russia in 1812 knew a soldier felt little pain when his legs were nearly frozen.

Chewing coca leaves brought welcome relief during trephinations, in which holes were drilled in the patient's head.

In 1867, British physician Sir Benjamin Ward Richardson chilled and deadened the skin with ether spray for small operations such as the removal of skin tumors and infections. But the sprays only deadened pain on or near the skin's surface. They did not have a deep, long-lasting effect on the nerves below the surface.

Surgeons needed an anesthetic that could work deep within the body to block out specific nerve centers—a local anesthetic. The drugs had to be liquid so they could be injected wherever they were needed. They also had to stop pain for a long period of time so surgeons could perform complicated operations. In the late 1800s, it was discovered that cocaine satisfied these requirements.

A Powerful Drug

Cocaine was not an unknown drug when it became popular as a local anesthetic. The people of South America had known for hundreds of years that chewing coca leaves brought relief from pain, particularly during trephinations. The South Americans did not know that cocaine, a bitter compound found in the coca leaves, is what made the pain disappear. They only knew the plant had the power to deaden pain.

In 1854, an Austrian naturalist who had gone to Peru to study plant and animal life brought dried coca leaves

Researchers learned the power of cocaine during their experiments. It could numb the nerves, affect heart rate and breathing, and bring on mood swings. It also proved to be dangerously addictive.

back to Europe for further study. Because the plant was unknown to European chemists, they were curious about its chemical makeup. In 1860, one young chemist, Albert Niemann, mixed ground coca leaves with water and alcohol. When the liquid evaporated, cocaine crystals formed.

Because the plant was called coca, Niemann called the colorless, four-to-six-sided crystals "cocaine." As part of his experiments, he tasted cocaine and reported that the bitter drug "numbs the nerves of the tongue, depriving it of feeling and taste."

During the next few years, physicians and researchers learned that cocaine was a powerful drug. In 1868, Peruvian army surgeon Moreno y Maiz injected cocaine into a frog's leg and operated on the nerve without hurting the frog.

Other researchers and physicians discovered that cocaine also affected a patient's heart rate and breathing and that it excited the brain and made a person feel happy and later depressed. These discoveries of how cocaine affected the inside of the body interested physicians more than the drug's ability to numb the body.

Sigmund Freud, a young Austrian physician who would become world famous for his work in psychoanalysis, a method of examining and treating emotional disorders, was interested in cocaine's effect on the brain. He also wondered if cocaine could cure the morphine addictions of some of his patients. He did not know then that cocaine was also addictive.

Freud invited Carl Koller, another young Austrian doctor, to work with him on his cocaine experiments. Freud and Koller had heard the rumors that the people of Peru could run long distances without tiring after they had chewed coca leaves. The young Austrians wanted to test their own strength while under the influence of cocaine. They swallowed some cocaine and then used a machine to measure the strength of their handgrip.

Freud and Koller's experiments taught them that cocaine made their tongues and throat numb, but they did

The Austrian doctor Sigmund Freud, best known for his work in psychoanalysis, noticed that cocaine had a numbing effect when swallowed.

not learn much else until Koller conducted some experiments of his own while Freud was out of town.

Numbing the Eye

Koller was studying to be an ophthalmologist, or eye doctor, and had been searching for a local anesthetic that would make painless eye surgery possible. Koller avoided ether and chloroform because the gases made patients vomit, and the strain on the eye that came with vomiting could damage an eye that had just undergone surgery. He also wanted his patients to be awake during surgery so they could follow his instructions.

Koller remembered that cocaine had made his mouth numb, and he wondered if it might also numb the eye's thin membranes. He decided to find out.

In an experiment, Koller put cocaine drops into a frog's eye and then touched the cornea, the clear membrane over the eye, with a pin. The frog did not blink or try to move away. When Koller touched the untreated eye, the frog jerked away. Next, Koller touched the anesthetized eye with sharp instruments, burning liquids, and an electrical current. The frog never flinched.

Koller trickled cocaine solution into his own eyes. He touched the head of a pin to his cornea and cried out, "I cannot feel anything." Koller knew cocaine was the anesthetic he had been looking for.

In September 1884, the Congress of Ophthalmology met in Germany. Koller could not afford to go, so he gave a friend a short research paper to read at the meeting and a vial of cocaine. The news of Koller's experiments and proof that cocaine did anesthetize eyes spread rapidly. His work opened up the new field of local anesthesia, and cocaine began to be more widely used.

Other doctors had also been looking for a powerful local anesthetic. Because cocaine can penetrate the thin, sensitive mucous membranes, the drug became the anesthetic of choice for surgeons operating on noses, mouths, and throats, which are all thickly lined with mucous membranes.

Injecting Cocaine

From their work with frogs and small animals, researchers knew cocaine numbed nerves but that it had no effect on the skin's tougher outside layer and could not penetrate it. Without a way to get the drug under the skin and to the nerves, doctors had limited use for cocaine as a local anesthetic.

Researchers, however, had two relatively new inventions available to them for getting cocaine under the skin. Charles Gabriel Pravaz of France had invented the hypodermic syringe in 1853, the same year Scottish physician

The hypodermic syringe and hollow needle allowed anesthesiologists to inject cocaine and other drugs under the skin.

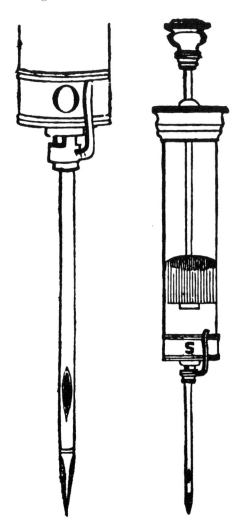

Alexander Wood had invented the hollow needle. The hollow needle could hold liquid drugs and pierce the skin, and the hypodermic syringe could draw the drugs into the needle and then slowly push them out. Used together, they made it possible for anesthesiologists to inject cocaine under the skin.

Within months of Koller's discovery, W.C. Burke, a Connecticut doctor, injected cocaine into a patient's hand to numb the nerves and block pain sensations from traveling to the brain. The patient had accidentally shot himself in the hand. By the time he came to Burke, his hand and fingers were swollen with infection. The ball of shot had to come out, but the incision would be painful.

Burke injected cocaine deep into the back of the hand. The injection hurt, and the man felt a burning sensation as the drug entered. Because the cocaine worked quickly on the nerves, the second injection along the little finger was painless. When the hand was numb, Burke made a deep, two-inch-long incision into the hand, took out the ball, and cleaned and dressed the wound.

Burke had performed minor surgery using cocaine injection, but he was only a local doctor and his work did not attract much notice. It was the work of the famous New York surgeon William S. Halsted later of Johns Hopkins Hospital in Maryland that made the medical community pay attention.

Nerve Blocks

Halsted made significant contributions to the field of local anesthesia. His research showed that to anesthetize the

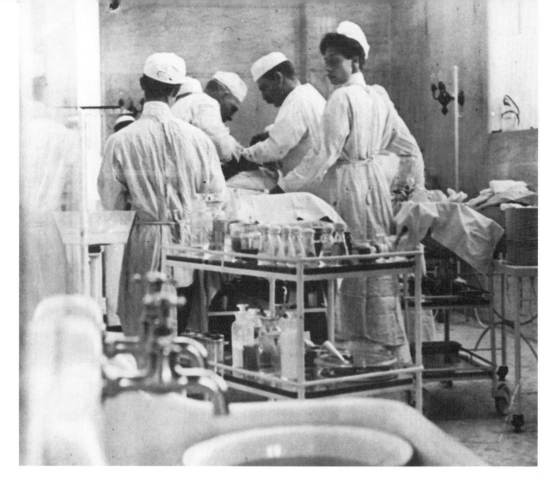

This early twentieth-century photo shows William S. Halsted operating on a patient.
Halsted used cocaine to block the nerves during surgery.

skin, the anesthetic must be injected directly into the skin, not under it. He also learned that most anesthesiologists were using stronger concentrations of the anesthetics than they needed. Cocaine in large doses was poisonous, and Halsted's work showed weaker doses still blocked pain.

Halsted also used local anesthesia in an entirely new way. While most researchers were still testing cocaine on mucous membranes, Halsted experimented with cocaine for complete nerve blocks in various parts of the body. He discovered that injections of cocaine around a nerve's main trunk could numb an entire region of the body, such as an arm, a leg, or the jaw.

This became known as neuro-regional anesthesia. By 1885, just a year after Koller's discovery, Halsted reported one thousand successful operations using cocaine as the local anesthetic, and he established the use of nerve blocks during surgery.

Unfortunately, the drug that established his reputation also led to his temporary downfall. During his experiments with cocaine, Halsted developed an addiction. For several years, he was unable to write about his many surgical discoveries, and much of his groundbreaking work with cocaine as an anesthetic at first went unnoticed by everyone except those who worked with him. Halsted struggled and finally won his battle against addiction, but he remained a living reminder of the drug's dark side.

Halsted's work with regional nerve blocks did not go unnoticed by Leonard Corning, a neurologist in New York. He probably attended Halsted's lectures and demonstrations there. Corning was not interested in cocaine injections for surgery but rather as therapy for nerve disorders and pain, which he thought originated along the spine.

In 1885, Corning wanted to see if he could use cocaine to anesthetize the spinal cord, so he injected the drug into the bloodstream near a dog's spine. Within five minutes, the dog lost control of its back legs and showed no response to pain. The dog's front legs, however, could move and feel pain, so Corning knew the cocaine had affected only the part of the body below the injection.

The Spinal Cord

Anesthesiologists give Corning the credit for administering the first epidural anesthesia, an injection near the spinal cord. Corning injected his cocaine just outside the dura, the fluid-filled sac that protects the spinal cord. Because he did not penetrate the dura, Corning did not perform true spinal anesthesia, but he showed that nerves branching off from the spinal cord could be anesthetized with cocaine.

Corning's epidural procedure provided a first step toward discovering spinal anesthesia. A German physician named Heinrich I. Quincke provided the next step.

In 1891, Quincke showed that the dura, the spinal cord's protective lining, could be punctured without damaging the cord. The dura contains spinal fluid, and Quincke wanted to penetrate the dura so he could draw out this fluid and study it to diagnose illness.

Quincke inserted a large needle low into the spine between the third and fourth vertebrae, or bony segments of the spine. Inserting the needle low in the back below the end of the spinal cord protected the spinal cord from damage. Quincke's technique, called the lumbar puncture method, started doctors thinking about puncturing the dura and injecting cocaine directly into the liquid surrounding the spinal cord.

Corning's curiosity about anesthetizing the spinal cord to control pain

Heinrich I. Quincke's development of the lumbar puncture technique spurred other scientists to experiment with spinal anesthesia.

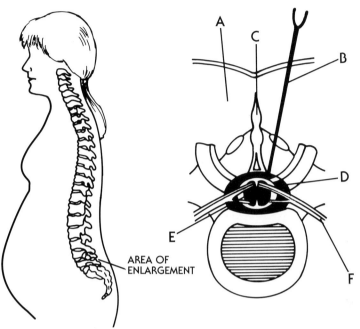

EPIDURAL ANESTHESIA

AREA OF ENLARGEMENT

A
C
B
D
E
F

Epidural anesthesia is often used during labor and childbirth because it enables the woman to remain conscious during the birth process.

In epidural anesthesia, the anesthetist pierces the back muscles (A) with a thin needle (B) and injects a local anesthetic into the space between the vertebra (C) and the dura (D), the protective sac surrounding the spinal cord (E). The local anesthetic deadens the nerves (F) as they branch off and leave the spinal cord, but it does not affect the spinal cord itself.

and Quincke's work with the lumbar puncture made it possible for German surgeon August Bier to put the anesthetizing powers of cocaine to work on the spine. The spine is one of the body's major nerve sites.

In 1898, using Quincke's lumbar puncture technique, Bier injected cocaine into the fluid surrounding a patient's spine. The lower half of the patient's body, just below the point of injection, was anesthetized for several hours. He successfully used spinal anesthesia on six other patients for operations to cure problems such as tuberculosis in the knee and ankle joints and compound fractures of the legs.

Bier wrote:

> These cases prove that when a relatively small amount of cocaine is injected into the [dura], large areas of the body can be made insensitive to pain and major operations can be performed.

Missing the Mark

Bier found, however, that these benefits came with a price. Patients complained of back and leg pain, vomiting, and in-

German surgeon August Bier discovered that by anesthetizing the spine, large areas of the body could be made insensitive to pain.

tense headaches, so Bier decided to have the procedure done on himself. This procedure was not successful.

After penetrating Bier's dura with a needle, the assistant was not able to attach the needle to the syringe containing the cocaine so the cocaine never reached the nerves. Bier lost a lot of spinal fluid through the puncture hole but never had a loss of feeling from the cocaine. The next day, he had a terrible headache. "I had the sensation of a very strong pressure in my head and felt dizzy when I arose quickly from my chair," Bier wrote. "I had to go to bed and stayed in bed for nine days."

Doctors now know that loss of spinal fluid can be followed by severe headaches. Even today, fear of headaches stops some people from choosing spinal anesthesia. Bier did not know then why he became ill. He suspected cocaine had been the problem and stopped administering spinal anesthesia for several years.

Because of his initial work, Bier is considered the discoverer of spinal anesthesia. In spite of the early problems, Bier's work encouraged others to use cocaine to anesthetize the spine. The method quickly spread from Europe to the United States, where doctors considered it to be a method with many advantages.

A Better Way

Spinal anesthesia killed pain long enough for major surgery, and it enabled surgeons to block many nerves at once. They could perform major operations without subjecting patients to the risks of inhalation anesthetics. It also allowed patients to stay awake. They did not have to fear going to sleep and waking up with nausea and a headache.

Because spinal anesthesia did not make patients vomit, it was especially good for emergency surgeries when the surgeon had to operate on someone who had just eaten and who could vomit and choke to death if made to breathe ether.

Less than twenty years after Koller introduced cocaine as a local anesthetic, spinal anesthesia was firmly established. Researchers continued to improve upon the method. Today, damage to the spinal cord is rare.

Since the late 1930s, various types of spinal blocks have been used as analgesics, or painkillers, to eliminate women's pain during childbirth. Local anesthetics can be dripped slowly into the spinal area through a thin plastic tube and can provide pain relief over

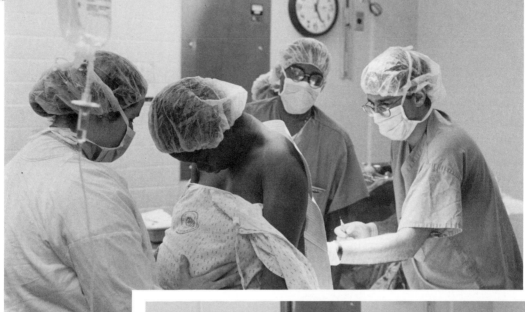

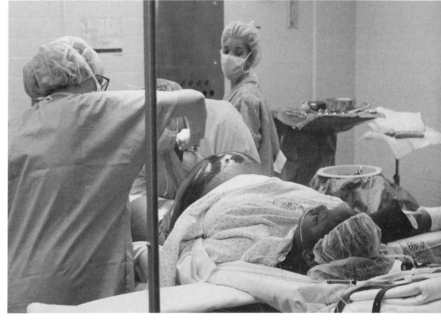

With modern anesthesia, cesarean deliveries are safe and pain free. An anesthetist administers an epidural anesthetic (above). Epidural anesthesia is so effective that the mother can remain awake while the baby is surgically removed (right).

many days. Today, spinal anesthesia is even used during cesarean deliveries when the baby must be surgically removed but the mother wants to watch the birth.

At about the time Corning and Quincke's experiments were taking place, Carl Ludwig Schleich was developing infiltration anesthesia, another method of local anesthesia.

In 1892, using a dilute solution of cocaine, morphine, and salt water,

Schleich demonstrated infiltration anesthesia to a group of German surgeons. He made several, closely spaced injections into the skin and saturated the tissues with cocaine. The anesthetic surrounded the area to be cut and numbed the tissues without the doctor having to go deeper for a nerve block. This weaker cocaine solution did not burn, so the patient felt no pain from the injection.

In the early 1900s, Schleich's infiltration anesthesia was used more often during surgery than any other form of local anesthesia. This easy method made doctors less nervous than the new method of spinal anesthesia with its possibility of headache and paralysis. Infiltration anesthesia was fast, and it was safer than ether or chloroform for many operations.

Surgeons still worried that these gases could harm their patients during surgery or give them lung and heart complications after surgery. Schleich wrote that if German surgeons used infiltration anesthesia for certain operations instead of the more dangerous gases one hundred German lives would be saved each year. Infiltration anesthesia, and the other local anesthetics for that matter, were still lacking in one important respect. They all relied on cocaine, and cocaine had significant shortcomings.

In doses large enough to be useful for prolonged anesthesia, cocaine was poisonous. During surgery, the drug caused sweating, vomiting, problems with blood circulation, and irregular heartbeats. After surgery, patients complained of headaches and blurred vision. Some patients died.

A Less Toxic Method

Researchers searched for ways to make the drug less toxic. German surgeon Heinrich Braun had used cocaine for local anesthesia and found he could make it less toxic and longer-lasting by mixing it with a hormone called epinephrine.

John Jacob Abel, an American professor of pharmacology, had isolated epinephrine in 1897. Epinephrine causes some blood vessels, particularly those in and under the skin, to contract. Epinephrine helps asthma sufferers by opening up their air passages and helping them breathe almost immediately. When used with local anesthetics, epinephrine helps reduce the loss of blood during minor surgeries.

When Braun injected a mixture of ephinephrine and cocaine, the mixture caused the blood vessels to tighten. This contraction slowed the absorption of cocaine into the body and prolonged cocaine's anesthetic effects without increasing its toxicity. But the addition of epinephrine did not eliminate cocaine's other major problems.

Cocaine, as Halsted's experience proved, was addictive, particularly in patients who received it more than once and in those who had it injected into the more sensitive spinal area. Imported from Bolivia and Peru and then processed in European laboratories, the drug was also expensive. Because heat caused cocaine to break down into other chemicals, the liquid could not be sterilized. This increased the risk of infection, particularly during spinal anesthesia when the entire spinal cord could become infected.

The drug's many problems encouraged chemists to find cocaine substitutes. Between the 1900s and 1930s, researchers and anesthesiologists looked for and found safer substitutes not only for cocaine but also for ether and chloroform. Their discoveries took anesthesia into the modern age.

Anesthesia Enters the Modern Age

Between 1900 and 1940, surgeons and anesthetists saw rapid advances in local anesthetics and in the general inhalation anesthetics that made a patient unconscious. Until the turn of the century, cocaine was the only effective local anesthetic, and ether and chloroform were the only general anesthetics strong enough to take a patient into deep surgical anesthesia.

Each of these anesthetics had drawbacks, so researchers worked to find replacements for cocaine and a wider selection of general anesthetic drugs. Their search led to three major discoveries.

In the early 1900s, chemists discovered they could combine chemicals similar to the ones found in cocaine to make a nonaddictive synthetic, or artificial, version of the drug. Chemists also

invented barbiturates. These synthetic drugs were used to calm or sedate patients and were eventually used for intravenous anesthesia.

Finally, the discovery of the gas cyclopropane in the 1930s expanded the choices of inhalation anesthetics and advanced the development of endotracheal anesthesia, the direct delivery of anesthetics into the lungs through a tube. Each of these improvements helped surgical anesthesia enter the modern age.

Synthetic Caines

The first of these three advances came in the late 1800s when Alfred Einhorn decided to find a cocaine substitute. Einhorn, considered one of the first

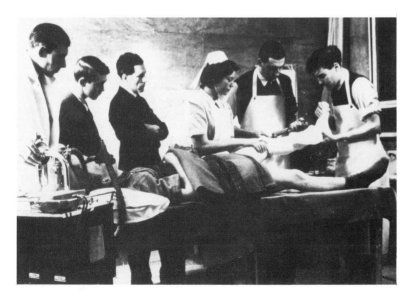

A photo from the early 1900s shows doctors setting a patient's fractured leg in a London hospital. The patient inhales anesthesia through a mask. Inhalation anesthetic techniques improved greatly in the early twentieth century.

pharmaceutical chemists, learned that when he heated cocaine and mixed it with mineral acids, the cocaine broke down into other chemicals.

Working in a laboratory in Munich, Germany, Einhorn isolated the different chemical groups in cocaine and then studied their effects on nerves and other tissues. He located the molecules, or groups of atoms, that caused anesthesia to occur. Using his knowledge of cocaine's chemical structure, Einhorn prepared many compounds that looked promising but failed to achieve the results of cocaine. Finally, in 1905, after twenty years of creating and testing various compounds, Einhorn developed procaine hydrochloride, the first effective synthetic cocaine.

It appears that Einhorn never published a report on his discovery. Instead, the world learned about procaine through the written reports of German surgeon Heinrich Braun. In 1905, Braun used Einhorn's procaine and found it to be an ideal, nonirritating local anesthetic. The effects of procaine, however, did not last long.

As he had with cocaine, Braun added epinephrine to procaine to prolong its anesthetic effects. In its longer-lasting form, procaine eventually came to be preferred for nerve blocks over the addictive and toxic cocaine.

During the next sixty years, a whole group of local anesthetics was synthesized, tested, and marketed. Most had the suffix *caine* in their names. Some were used as spinal anesthetics. Some had only a short-term effect. Some only worked on the surface of the skin, and others did not work unless they were injected deep into the tissues.

Each synthetic drug had its own specific chemical makeup, but all of them gave doctors what they had been looking for—relatively safe, effective substitutes for cocaine that would block pain in the area of the operation without making the patient unconscious.

None, however, were as widely used as procaine, which carried the trade name of Novocain. This local anesthetic had the same pain-blocking effect as cocaine, was much less toxic to the body, and could be used in many different

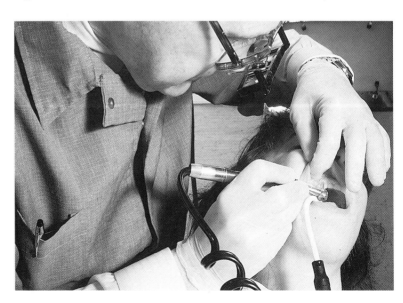

Early twentieth-century researchers found ways to imitate cocaine's nerve-blocking abilities without passing on its harmful side effects. These local anesthetics are often used in dentistry.

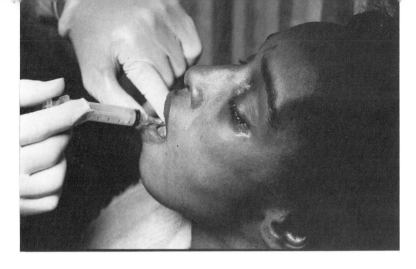

Some local anesthetics work only if they are injected. Here, a dentist injects an anesthetic into a patient's gum.

types of operations. Because of these advantages, Novocain remained the most widely used local anesthetic for many years. Around 1950, lidocaine, an improved version, was introduced. It continues to be used today.

A New Class of Drugs

At about the same time that Einhorn was creating a cocaine substitute, other German chemists were researching another synthetic. In 1903, Emil Fischer and Joseph von Mering synthesized barbital and developed the new class of drugs known as barbiturates. The names of these drugs often end with the *al* suffix.

At first, these drugs were used only to relax patients or to put them to sleep before surgery. Many patients were frightened when the mask needed for ether or chloroform was put on. Their fears often grew with the choking sensations they felt before the gas made them unconscious. Many patients struggled and tried to pull off the mask. Doctors found it was easier to put the anesthesia mask on a patient after an injection of a barbiturate had put the person to sleep.

Because barbital worked quickly to calm a patient, the drug proved to be a good sedative. Because the drug took too long to reach maximum effectiveness and then took too long to wear off, it was not a good general anesthetic. Some of the early barbiturates kept patients asleep for days. Prolonged sleeps with little motion encouraged pneumonia and general weakness.

Anesthetists decided to experiment with shortening the barbiturates' effect so that the drugs could be used not

Emil Fischer is one of two men who developed a new class of drugs known as barbiturates.

ANESTHESIA AND THE HUMAN NERVOUS SYSTEM

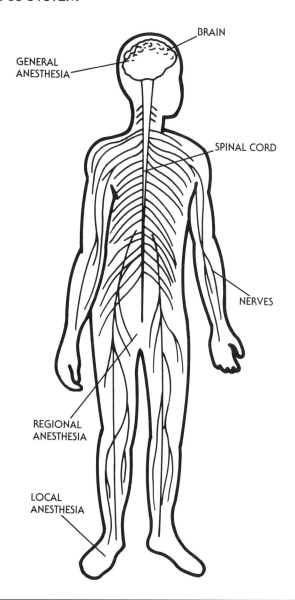

Pain messages travel in the human body over billions of nerve cells. These nerve cells connect with the brain and spinal cord, forming a network called the nervous system. The nervous system sends messages to and from the brain through main nerve trunks that extend to the arms, legs, neck and head, skin, and organs.

Anesthesia—whether local, regional, or general—stops pain messages from reaching the brain. Local anesthesia numbs the nerves inside a small area of the body such as a part of a foot or hand. Regional anesthesia blocks large groups of nerves or the spinal cord to eliminate pain in larger regions of the body. With both local and regional anesthesia, the numbed nerves in the anesthetized area prevent pain messages from traveling to the brain while other nerves continue to function normally.

Under general anesthesia, which is used for major operations such as heart surgery, pain messages from all over the body are halted. General anesthesia makes the patient temporarily unconscious so that the brain receives no pain messages or sensations from the nervous system.

only as sedatives but also as general anesthetics during surgery. Research with longer-acting barbiturates opened up the field of intravenous anesthesia in the 1920s. After inhalation and local anesthesia, intravenous anesthesia was an important discovery.

Through the Bloodstream

With intravenous anesthesia, the patient receives the general anesthetic through a vein rather than through the lungs, as in inhalation anesthesia. In both cases, however, the blood carries the liquid or gaseous drug to the brain, which controls the body's nervous system.

For many years, doctors and researchers had experimented with intravenous methods to stop pain. In the seventeenth century, Christopher Wren, a famous London architect and scientist, used a hollow quill to put opium directly into a dog's bloodstream. Wren was looking for ways to relieve pain rather than for ways to cause surgical anesthesia, but his work was some of the first research into intravenous anesthesia.

Doctors thought they had found the perfect intravenous anesthetic when hexobarbital was introduced in Germany in 1932. Evipal, as the drug was called, was the first short-acting intravenous anesthetic. The drug was well received by doctors everywhere because it caused unconsciousness faster than any other anesthetic on the market.

Patients also liked the drug's quick action. One story tells of a wealthy British businessman, Lord Nuffield, who received Evipal before an operation. When he awoke, he glanced at his watch and asked why the operation had not started. When he was told the operation was over, Lord Nuffield declared the operation a "magic experience" and later donated a large sum of money to Oxford University to support the study of anesthetics.

Instant Sleep

Researchers, however, kept looking for better barbiturates that would work even faster. In 1934, they introduced thiopental sodium, or sodium Pentothal, as it came to be known. This faster-acting solid drug is dissolved in sterile water before it is injected into the veins. Stronger and faster than Evipal, Pentothal quickly became popular as an intravenous anesthetic. Its effects are almost instantaneous. Before a patient can count to ten, the drug causes sleep and even makes a patient forget the entire procedure. Patients also wake up quickly after the surgery, even though they feel sleepy for a longer time.

The drug worked well for extremely long procedures because its effects could be maintained by several injections spaced out during the surgery. Pentothal also stopped vomiting and nausea, two of inhalation anesthesia's most unpleasant aftereffects.

Negative Effects

Over time, however, the negative side effects not only of Pentothal but of all the intravenous barbiturates became known. These drugs, researchers learned, were not safe for everyone. Patients with heart or lung problems, for example, had to avoid barbiturates because they slowed the heart and breathing rates and affected circulation and blood pressure.

There was another important problem with barbiturates. Barbiturates did not give doctors the same control they had with anesthetic gases, which enter and leave the body with each breath the patient takes. With barbiturates, the patient received an injection directly into the blood. The drug had to run its course through the bloodstream, even if the patient could not tolerate the barbiturate and had a bad reaction.

Although some of the short-acting barbiturates quickly left the bloodstream, a good amount was stored in the body's tissues. The body readily absorbs barbiturates and releases the drugs slowly back into the body, causing bouts of sleepiness days after the injection.

Today, barbiturates are rarely used as the only general anesthetic during surgery. In the past fifty years, more than twenty-five hundred barbiturates have been synthesized. Most often, they are used in combination with local or general anesthetics during surgery or as chemical aids that help a patient relax or fall asleep before surgery.

Barbiturates are also used in sleeping pills. Because they are addictive and can cause death when taken with alcohol or in large amounts, barbiturates must be prescribed by a doctor.

Safer Gases

The introduction in the 1930s of intravenous anesthesia did not keep researchers from also looking for better and safer gases. Several gases were discovered and used before the mid-1900s. Cyclopropane, however, was the most successful and was used widely for several decades.

Like many of the anesthetic drugs, cyclopropane was not an unknown gas when doctors first decided to try it. Chemists had discovered the gas in their laboratories in the late 1800s, but they were not looking for an anesthetic gas. It took almost another forty years and an accident for researchers to look at cyclopropane as a possible anesthetic.

In 1929, Canadian researchers had been experimenting with propylene as a possible anesthetic gas. This gas worked when it was freshly prepared, but when stored in a steel cylinder, it quickly deteriorated into a toxic substance that caused nausea and irregular heartbeats.

The chemists identified this toxic substance as cyclopropane. They did not know if cyclopropane could be adapted for use as an anesthetic but decided to go on with the work anyway. Because they knew that oxygen made the anesthetic gases work more effectively, they mixed a small amount of cyclopropane with oxygen and gave it to two kittens. The animals quietly fell asleep, and then awoke easily when the gas was removed.

The researchers experimented with cyclopropane on themselves and proved it was safe for humans when used in small amounts and when mixed with oxygen. The Canadian government, however, stopped them from using it on patients. Three people had died in Toronto while inhaling a different anesthetic, and the officials were concerned this new gas would bring even more deaths.

Rather than let the cyclopropane research die, the Canadian researchers asked their American colleagues at the University of Wisconsin to continue the experiments on human subjects. American researchers, guided by physician Ralph Waters, agreed to do the work. By 1935, cyclopropane was being used in surgery. Many considered it an ideal general anesthetic with many advantages.

Deep Anesthesia

First, cyclopropane appeared to have no ill effects on the brain, heart, liver, or kidneys, and it swiftly disappeared from the patient's system. The researchers also found that only a small amount of cyclopropane is needed to cause deep surgical anesthesia.

The gas mixture needs to be only 12 to 20 percent cyclopropane to cause deep anesthesia. As a result, the patient can breathe plenty of life-sustaining oxygen and still be unconscious. Because it works well with a high mixture of oxygen, cyclopropane is safer for lengthy surgeries because the patient's system is not deprived of normal oxygen levels.

The gas also works quickly and can put a patient deeply asleep in less than two minutes. In contrast, ether takes from ten to thirty minutes to put a patient into surgical anesthesia.

Unlike ether, cyclopropane has a powerful effect on the central nervous system. This ability to depress, or quiet, the nerves helps cyclopropane relax the abdominal muscles, which ether does not do. The abdominal muscles must be relaxed or surgeons struggle to get

their hands past the rigid muscle walls and into the body's cavity.

Cyclopropane is also more pleasant to breathe than ether, so patients do not struggle against the mask, and they wake as from a normal sleep without feeling nauseated. It does not irritate the lungs or throat and does not cause an increase in saliva or mucus, which could travel into the lungs and cause choking. The gas also causes the patient to breathe quietly and shallowly, so it is ideal for operations on the heart, lungs, or chest when the surgeon needs the chest to be as still as possible.

A High Price

In spite of cyclopropane's many benefits, it is not the perfect general anesthetic. Because the gas slows a patient's breathing, even the slightest overdose

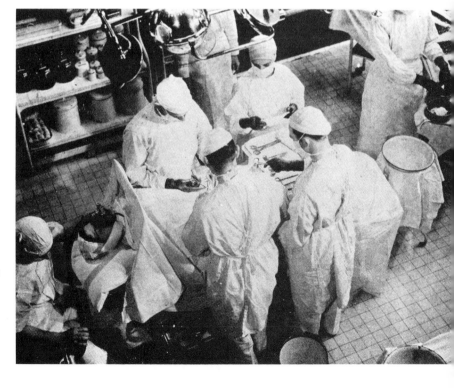

A photo of a patient undergoing an operation. Since the 1930s when intravenous anesthesia was introduced, doctors have continued to adapt and refine anesthetic gases to make them safer and more effective.

BREATHING APPARATUS

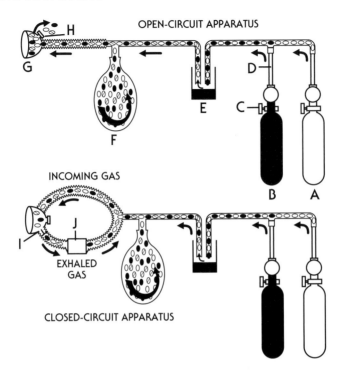

OPEN-CIRCUIT APPARATUS

INCOMING GAS

EXHALED GAS

CLOSED-CIRCUIT APPARATUS

Anesthetic machines have changed a great deal over the years, but most are based on one of two designs. The most basic machine, introduced in 1917, has an open circuit which allows excess anesthetic gases to escape into the air. The closed-circuit or rebreathing machine is more sophisticated in that it recycles expensive anesthetic gases rather than allowing them to escape.

Both systems combine measured amounts of oxygen and nitrogen with an anesthetic gas such as ether or halothane. Oxygen is contained in one cylinder (A) and nitrogen in another (B). Each cylinder is equipped with a valve (C) for controlling flow and a flowmeter (D) for measuring it. A third container (E) holds the anesthetic. Once released, all three mix in the reservoir bag (F). When the patient inhales through the mask (G), the gas mixture travels from the bag into the patient's lungs.

In an open-circuit system, the patient exhales through a valve, called an expiratory valve (H). The exhaled breath is released into the air. It contains carbon dioxide which is expelled during normal breathing. It also contains excess anesthetic gases, which are costly as well as unusable once they are released.

The closed-circuit or rebreathing system captures and reuses these excess gases. When the patient exhales, the carbon dioxide and excess anesthetic cycle back into the breathing system through a one-way valve called a non-return valve (I). The gases pass through a chamber (J) which absorbs and holds the carbon dioxide. The exhaled anesthetic gases, cleaned of carbon dioxide, return to the reservoir bag and then flow back to the patient.

of this potent drug can stop breathing altogether. Although the gas does not slow the heart, it can disturb the body's circulation and force an already weak heart to pump even harder.

The gas's ability to bring deep muscle relaxation also comes at a price, for this level of relaxation happens only when this extremely powerful gas is used at near-overdose concentrations. Sometimes, this level of relaxation cannot be maintained without causing an irregular heartbeat.

In the hands of skilled and experienced anesthetists, cyclopropane is an excellent anesthetic gas. The doctors, however, must have sensitive equipment that accurately measures how much cyclopropane a patient is receiving. The doctor must closely watch the patient's heart rate and breathing and be ready to use artificial respiration to help the lungs keep working should the patient's breathing suddenly stop.

In addition to the risk of overdose, cyclopropane has two other disadvantages that eventually kept it out of operating rooms. The gas is flammable and highly explosive, and it is expensive.

The risk of explosion is very real in operating rooms where equipment can cause sparks that ignite flammable gases. Hospitals solved most of the problems with explosions by putting humidifiers and non-static floor and wall coverings in operating rooms. These changes helped reduce hazards from electrical sparks.

New Ideas

Researchers helped to make the gas less expensive by finding ways to recycle it. When people breathe normally, they in-hale oxygen and exhale the poisonous gas carbon dioxide. Patients under anesthesia inhale oxygen mixed with anesthetic gases and exhale the anesthetics along with the carbon dioxide. With each breath, the patient inhales a fresh mixture of anesthetic gas and oxygen.

Ralph Waters at the University of Wisconsin lessened the cost of using fresh gas by attaching a carbon dioxide absorber to the breathing equipment. The absorber removed the carbon dioxide from each exhaled breath and returned the cyclopropane to the patient's lungs. By reusing the cyclopropane, anesthetists could cut their costs.

After the problems of explosions and expense were taken care of, doctors still faced the danger that a patient could overdose and stop breathing. Because of this disadvantage, however, to use this gas safely, anesthetists had to become more skilled at endotracheal anesthesia. This was an important advance.

Into the Lungs

During endotracheal anesthesia, the anesthetic gas is delivered directly into a patient's lungs through a tube inserted into the trachea, or windpipe, and down to the point where the lungs branch off. The tube is attached to the anesthesia machine, which pumps a mixture of gas and oxygen directly into the lungs. This technique increases the amount of lung area the gas reaches, it provides a completely open airway into the lungs, and it protects the lungs from unwanted mouth and throat secretions.

Getting a tube of any kind past the

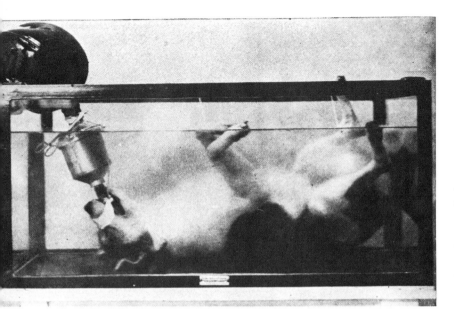

Arthur E. Guedel's dog Airway sleeps soundly while submerged in a tank of water. An endotracheal tube and anesthesia machine expel carbon dioxide and deliver anesthetics during the experiment.

sensitive larynx, or vocal cords, and into the throat is difficult. The larynx quickly contracts when touched, closing off the airway, and the patient gags and chokes. Local anesthetics that numb the throat and let the tube slip in easily made endotracheal anesthesia a little easier to perform.

The method, however, still required some skill and experience, so many doctors hesitated to try it. Many were not even sure it worked. In 1928, Arthur E. Guedel, a young physician, researcher, and inventor, improved upon the ordinary endotracheal tube by attaching a soft rubber cuff to its top end. The cuff helped seal any air leaks between the tube and the throat.

The Dunked-Dog Experiment

With this new endotracheal tube, Guedel performed one of the most spectacular animal experiments ever done. Guedel and his dog, Airway, proved endotracheal anesthesia was both safe and effective. Guedel submerged Airway in a tank of water. The little dog's muzzle was taped shut and in his mouth was a small, cuffed tube. The tube was attached to a small anesthesia machine that pumped gas into the dog's lungs and removed its carbon dioxide through the absorber Waters had invented.

People watched in amazement as Airway slept submerged under water for four hours. Then, Guedel lifted Airway out of the tank and pulled the tube out of his windpipe. Slowly, Airway opened his eyes, wagged his tail, feebly tried to shake himself dry, and then laid back down for a nap. Guedel and Airway proved that endotracheal anesthesia could deliver anesthetics safely and continually through an open airway.

Endotracheal anesthesia also showed thoracic, or chest, surgeons that it was safe to open a patient's chest. Surgeons had avoided thoracic surgery because

ENDOTRACHEAL TUBE

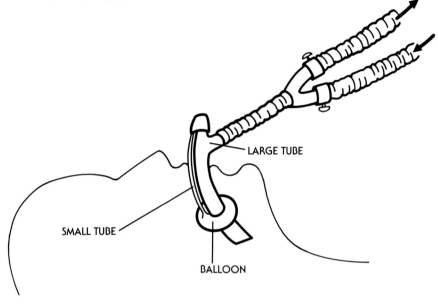

LARGE TUBE

SMALL TUBE

BALLOON

The endotracheal tube made anesthesia more effective and safe. When inserted into a patient's trachea, or windpipe, the endotracheal tube allows anesthesia to flow directly into the lungs. The tube also prevents foreign matter, such as mucous or blood, from entering the windpipe and choking the patient.

The endotracheal tube actually consists of two tubes, one larger than the other. Anesthetic gas flows through the large tube into the patient's lungs. The smaller tube is attached to a small, doughnut-shaped balloon that surrounds the larger tube.

When the anesthetist inserts the endotracheal tube into the windpipe the balloon is in a collapsed or deflated position. Once the tube is in position, the anesthetist inflates it through the small tube.

The inflated balloon hugs the walls of the throat and forms a perfect seal against secretions. The inflated balloon is not strong enough to close off the endotracheal tube, so anesthetic gases can still flow from the anesthesia machine to the lungs and exhaled gases can return to the machine.

the lungs collapsed with the change in internal body pressure that came when the chest was opened. A patient could not live without working lungs. An endotracheal tube and breathing machine, however, are able to take over for the lungs, and they made chest surgeries possible.

Endotracheal anesthesia also opened the door to the next revolution in anesthesia—the use of the powerful drug curare. Curare plus the discovery of a new family of anesthetic gases gave doctors a wider range of choices when they tried to select the best anesthetics for each patient.

More Choices, Safer Anesthesia

The last major drug advances in surgical anesthesia came from two unlikely places: the jungles of South America and the World War II testing labs for the atomic bomb. The drug curare (pronounced ku-rar-ee) and the gas halothane complete the list of drugs anesthetists can choose from to make surgery safer for patients.

Richard C. Gill urged researchers to test curare as a possible cure for the multiple sclerosis that crippled his body.

Curare's mysteries go back hundreds of years, but the drug's modern story began in 1934 with Richard C. Gill, an American who had lived in the jungles of Ecuador. He lay in a hospital bed in Washington, D.C., and could move only his head. The rest of his body suffered from muscle spasms and paralysis. The doctors told him he had multiple sclerosis, a nerve disorder. They said he would never recover.

"The Flying Death"

Gill had built his life around travel and adventure, and he refused to believe his active days were over. He decided to beat this illness with curare, a jungle drug called "the flying death." He knew curare had a powerful effect on muscles; perhaps, it could make his work again.

He could not know then that his dream to be well and his decision to find and bring back curare would dramatically change medicine. In fact, curare ranks second only to ether in the impact it has had on surgery and anesthesia.

Made from the sap of the liana, a jungle vine, curare is a deadly and frightening poison. The Indians of Ecuador and Peru coated their arrows with curare, and any animal or person they wounded dropped within moments. The poison did not kill directly. Instead, it paralyzed the muscles, including the

South American Indians coated the tips of their hunting arrows with the poison curare. The gourd at left held this poison. (Below) South American Indians prepare the jungle plant poison that they will use for hunting.

diaphragm, the muscle that makes breathing possible. The wounded animal or person, unable to move and then unable to breathe, suffocated.

When he lived in Ecuador, Gill had earned the Indians' trust, and when they made him an honorary witch doctor, he was allowed to watch them prepare curare. He decided to make some and to give it to American researchers so they could learn how to use it to conquer multiple sclerosis.

Gill exercised tirelessly to regain control of his crippled body. In 1938, he arrived in Ecuador. Limping, using a cane, relying on the Indians to help him, he stayed in the jungles for five months gathering liana. He prepared the poison himself so he could be sure of its purity.

He brought twenty-five pounds of

curare to the United States and then tried to convince drug companies to invest in curare research. The companies needed to know there was a use for curare before they spent money to produce it. They did not believe anyone would buy a drug that suffocated people, so they refused Gill's request.

Unlocking the Muscles

Gill was disheartened until a letter from A.E. Bennett, a professor of neurology and psychiatry at the University of Nebraska, rekindled hope. Bennett said he wanted to use curare on people who were paralyzed. Gill's samples would be enough for his experiments.

Bennett injected measured amounts of curare into patients whose arms and legs were twisted with paralysis. Curare did unlock the muscles but only for a short time. When the drug wore off, the paralysis returned.

Gill had hoped Bennett's research would eventually cure his own muscle disorder. It never did. Once again, he was disappointed. Bennett, however, was not. He saw possible uses for curare with patients undergoing drug or electrical shock therapy for mental illness.

Shock therapy helped some patients but at a high price. The shocks caused convulsions and spasms so violent that patients often dislocated joints, broke arms and legs, and sometimes fractured their spines. Bennett injected curare just before the shock therapy began. He gave just enough to quiet the muscles without stopping breathing. The curare kept the bones from breaking.

News of Bennett's important work spread in the medical community and kept interest in curare alive. Lewis

A.E. Bennett, a professor of neurology and psychiatry at the University of Nebraska, saw the advantages of using curare as a muscle relaxant.

Wright, an anesthesiologist who already knew a lot about curare, was interested in Bennett's experiments.

Bennett's work showed Wright that curare, when carefully measured, could be used safely in humans to relax muscles. Wright was interested in relaxing muscles during surgery. He knew that to relax muscles enough for abdominal surgery, dangerously high levels of anesthetics were needed—more than the amount needed to cause unconsciousness. Wright wondered if curare could be used to relax muscles during surgery.

Wright took his idea to an old friend, Canadian surgeon Harold Griffith. A practical man with years of surgical experience, Griffith believed in trying new things. He had been the second doctor to start using cyclopropane when the gas was released for use.

Griffith could see the advantages of quieting muscles with curare rather than with high levels of general anesthesia that stressed organs and caused circulation problems. Fears that curare would suffocate patients did not alarm him.

Unlike most surgeons in the 1940s, Griffith was experienced with endotracheal anesthesia. Because he used cyclopropane, a gas that could stop a patient's breathing, Griffith always put a breathing tube down his patients' throats as a precaution and attached it to a ventilator, or breathing machine. If the curare did paralyze the diaphragm, he knew he could keep his patient breathing. He decided to give the drug a try.

"The Easiest Abdominal Operation"

In Montreal, Canada, on January 23, 1942, Griffith injected curare into a young patient about to have an appen-dectomy, a procedure to remove the appendix, a small piece of intestine. Griffith's curare came from Gill's samples. Working as the anesthesiologist, Griffith slowly reduced the flow of cyclopropane into the patient's lungs until he knew he did not have enough gas to keep the muscles relaxed. The curare, however, had taken effect.

The twenty-seven-year-old surgeon, George T. Novinger, easily parted the strong and usually rigid stomach muscles. Novinger said later that it was "the easiest abdominal operation I have done in my short career."

The operation went well. The oxygen flowing through the endotracheal tube supported the patient's breathing, and the curare wore off after about twenty minutes. No one in the operating room realized they had started the next revolution in anesthesia.

Curare's ability to completely relax the muscles made toxic levels of anesthetics unnecessary. Anesthetists started giving patients just enough anesthetic to make them unconscious and let curare take care of relaxing the muscles.

Curare was especially useful for pa-

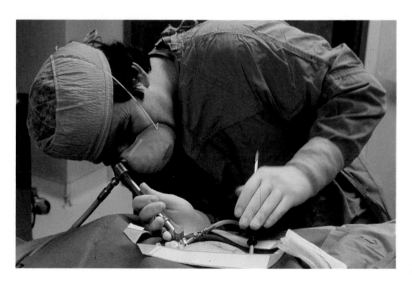

Surgeons must carefully part the rigid muscles of the stomach during appendectomies and other operations in the region of the stomach and abdomen. Curare relaxed the muscles and thus made the surgeon's job easier.

tients who could not tolerate heavy doses of inhalation anesthetics. Many old people, small children, or those already weakened by illness could not survive toxic levels of general anesthetic, but they could tolerate just enough to put them to sleep.

The News Spreads

News of curare spread quickly. By the end of World War II, it was used in thousands of operations. When researchers finally isolated the chemical in curare that makes it effective, mass production of the drug became possible. Researchers now knew the exact chemicals they needed to make the drug.

Surgeons also experimented with larger doses of curare and found that an increase improved not only muscle relaxation but also patient recovery. When they are spared the toxic effects of heavy doses of anesthesia, patients do not experience nausea or headaches. Instead, they are able to sit up, take a few steps, and regain their strength.

Curare also made advanced surgical procedures possible. By keeping muscles perfectly still for hours without stressing the body, curare made intricate and long surgeries like today's heart and kidney transplants possible.

Curare is still harvested in the Amazon region, but today, anesthetists also use succinylcholine, a synthetic version of curare. Succinylcholine wears off quickly, so it is gradually dripped into the patient's veins throughout surgery. The synthetic gives continual muscle relaxation and more control to anes-

Once curare relaxed the muscles, they could remain very still for hours. This allowed surgeons to perform complex and long operations including heart and kidney transplants.

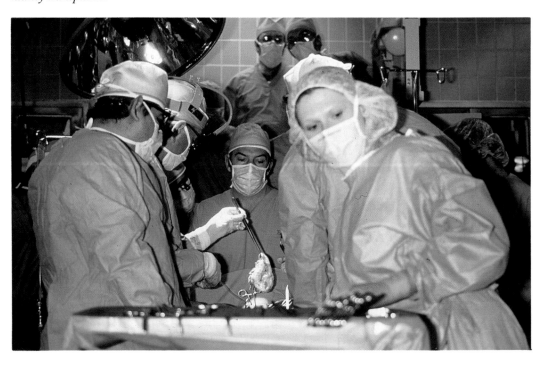

thetists because they can stop the drug's effects within seconds. Now "the flying death" brings safer anesthesia and life to millions.

Curare became commonplace in every operating room at about the same time researchers were busily experimenting with halothane, an entirely new anesthetic gas. Anesthetists hoped halothane would be the first potent, nonexplosive gaseous anesthetic.

Through the 1940s, all the anesthetics strong enough to cause deep, surgical anesthesia were explosive and potentially dangerous, even when used cautiously. Chloroform, the only nonexplosive inhalant, caused liver damage and affected the heart, so doctors had all but stopped using it. Nitrous oxide was not explosive, but it did not cause deep, surgical anesthesia.

The Manhattan Project

The door to finding a nonexplosive, potent inhalant anesthetic opened in 1943 when the U.S. government began the Manhattan Project, a secret experiment to build the first atomic bomb. To make this nuclear weapon, the atomic researchers needed refined uranium, a radioactive metal. They found they could separate uranium atoms, or the tiny bits of matter they needed for their research, if they first mixed uranium and fluorine, a poisonous, pale yellow gas.

This was not the first time anesthesiology researchers had been interested in fluorine. In the 1930s, they had studied fluorine as a possible ingredient in an anesthetic. They believed fluorine could combine with hydrogen and carbon—the explosive elements in anesthetics—to make them nonexplosive. The researchers were not successful in finding a new anesthetic, but their knowledge of anesthetics and fluorine enabled two of these researchers to make an accurate prediction:

> A survey of the properties of the 166 known gases suggested that the best possibility of finding a new, noncombustible anesthetic gas lay in the field of fluoride compounds.

The Manhattan Project put fluorine in the spotlight again. Part of the project's fluorine work was done by Earl T. McBee of Purdue University in Indiana. McBee was interested in adding fluorine to hydrogen and carbon to keep these chemical substances from exploding.

A manufacturer of anesthetics had previously given McBee money to test nonexplosive fluorinated compounds as anesthetics. McBee's work with the Manhattan Project helped speed up his work with fluorinated compounds. By the end of the war in 1945, McBee and his team had created tiny amounts of forty-six fluorinated gases.

During the next few years, American researchers tested dozens of hydrocarbons—compounds containing only hydrogen and carbon—as potential anesthetics. Their colleagues in Great Britain, however, tried a more direct approach. Rather than look for hydrocarbons to test, British chemist Charles Suckling asked anesthetists to describe their ideal anesthetic.

Their descriptions helped Suckling eliminate possible substances. An ideal anesthetic, they said, must not ignite, it must be potent enough to cause deep sleep, it must not explode, and it must evaporate well so that it is easy to give and is quickly taken into the lungs.

MEASURING AND MONITORING

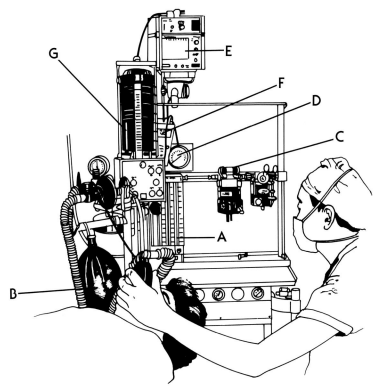

Modern anesthesia machines carefully measure the amount of anesthetic given to a patient. They also give the anesthetist important information about the patient's body and how it is functioning while under anesthesia.

As the patient breathes the anesthetic gases, flowmeters (A) accurately measure the amount of gas that enters the reservoir bag (B) each minute. Vaporizers (C) moisten the gases on their way to the lungs because moist air is easier to breathe than dry air.

The machine's blood pressure measurement (D) tells the anesthetist if the blood is circulating properly. The electocardiograph (E) shows if the heart is beating regularly, and the oxygen analyzer (F) tells the anesthetist exactly how much life-giving oxygen is in the bloodstream. If heart or lung function falters during surgery the machine's mechanical ventilator (G) will even take over a patient's breathing.

The Perfect Anesthetic

In 1956, using his expert understanding of known gases and their chemical properties, Suckling created halothane. He first tested halothane on houseflies before other researchers tested it on larger animals and finally on humans.

By the late 1950s, halothane was used in surgery and was thought to be the perfect anesthetic because it met every need. Simple to give with modern equipment, it could be delivered in precise amounts with safety and ease.

Halothane evaporated easily, was not flammable when mixed with oxygen, and would not explode. More potent than ether or chloroform, halothane quickly made patients unconscious and relaxed their muscles.

Patients came out of halothane anesthesia quickly and did not experience heavy salivation, vomiting, or heart problems. The gas did bring a drop in blood pressure, and high concentrations stopped a patient's breathing, but these conditions were either easily controlled or quickly reversed with modern equipment.

Within a few years, halothane was used in 80 percent of all cases in which general anesthesia was administered in the United States. In five years, it had been given to more than six million people.

Problems Surface

Within a few years, however, doctors began to notice a higher rate of liver damage among patients who had received halothane. The doctors suspected halothane damaged the liver by reducing the flow of blood to that organ. They also suspected halothane broke down in the body into toxic waste products, known as metabolites, that collected in the liver and damaged it. Researchers wanted to know how halothane was affecting the body.

The National Halothane Study was organized to study the drug's effect on the liver. Researchers examined the records of about 800,000 patients. They found that only 82 patients, or 1 in 10,000, had suffered liver damage. In all but 9 of the cases, the patients had developed liver problems before they inhaled halothane. Liver damage, the study said, was more likely to occur in patients who had received halothane more than once in the same month or in consecutive months.

Although the number of people hurt by halothane was small, anesthetists began using the gas less often. By 1965, researchers had created a substitute for halothane, called isoflurane. Isoflurane does not break down into toxic waste products as does halothane. In fact, most of the isoflurane that enters the body is safely exhaled unchanged through the breath.

Today, gases like isoflurane are preferred over halothane, but the research and discoveries that halothane triggered are a milestone in the history of anesthesia. By applying what they had learned about halothane, researchers

Anesthetists can choose from many types and methods of anesthesia today. This is essential for the many complex operations performed.

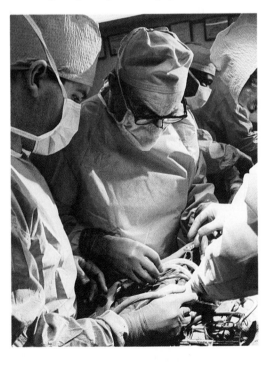

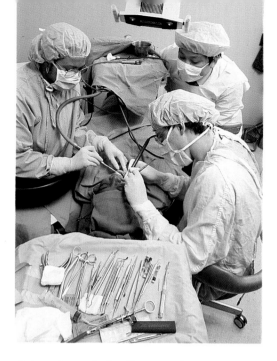

Balanced anesthesia allows anesthetists to combine various anesthetics and drugs to obtain the best effect.

during an operation, and they are able to select just the right combination of drugs for each patient.

This approach, which is called balanced anesthesia, became firmly established in the 1950s. The idea of using more than one drug during surgery began in 1908 when George W. Crile, a well-known surgeon in Cleveland, Ohio, used procaine in operations in which the patient already was receiving a general anesthetic. Crile believed nerves at the site of an operation experienced shock even if the unconscious patient appeared to feel nothing.

Crile's pioneering work led to today's balanced anesthesia approach, in which doctors use a wide range of drugs and take advantage of the best qualities of each. They use a drug to cause drowsiness and another to relax the patient before surgery. They select a painkiller during the operation, another drug to relax the muscles, and still another to cause unconsciousness.

This combination of several drugs is much easier on the patient's body. No one drug has to be used in amounts large enough to be poisonous. By having more choices, anesthetists can make surgical anesthesia safer for all patients.

The safety record of anesthetists is good. Each year in the United States, they perform more than twenty-five million anesthetic procedures. Of the millions of people who have received an anesthetic during the past twenty years, few have died.

Researchers continue to study anesthetics to make them even safer. Knowing more about anesthetics and how they work and one day finding the perfect anesthetic are the goals of people working in the field of surgical anesthesia.

were able to develop safer fluorinated anesthetics. Because these gases did not explode, they increased the safety in operating rooms. Because these newer anesthetics did not break down into metabolites that harmed the body, they were also safer for the patients who inhaled them.

Researchers continue to refine the fluorinated gases. Sevoflurane is now being tested in the United States and has been used in Japan since 1990. Desflurane, another gas, is being tested in Japan. If these fluorinated anesthetics pass rigorous testing and examination, one day they may be used by anesthetists worldwide.

Every anesthetic has advantages and disadvantages, and depending on the patient and the type of surgery, each entails some risk. But being anesthetized is much safer than it was even ten years ago. Today, anesthetists can use more than one type of anesthetic

CHAPTER 7

A Look into Anesthesia's Future

Anesthesia's future, like its past, most likely includes years with steady progress mixed with years of sudden, surprising change. Researchers probably will accomplish a great deal in the years ahead. They are likely to learn more about how anesthetic drugs work and how to ease or stop pain without drugs.

Anesthesia research will bring better drugs, better methods, and better equipment, in addition to better ways to use the drugs and machines that already exist. Anesthetic drugs may also be used by doctors to cure illness and disease unrelated to surgery and anesthesia.

Finally, and probably most important, anesthesia research may lead to the conquest of all pain, not just the surgical pain that made patients scream in operating rooms many years ago.

Body Chemistry

Anesthetists still do not know exactly how anesthetic drugs keep people from feeling pain or how these drugs can

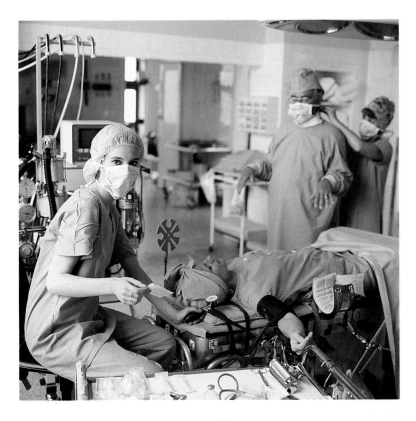

Anesthesia has changed the face of modern surgery. Nevertheless, researchers will continue to look for even better methods of administering surgical anesthesia.

make a person slip into unconsciousness. Learning how these drugs work inside the body, however, is only a small part of what scientists still must learn about the human body and how it functions.

Scientists still do not completely understand body chemistry. They do not understand exactly how the body's chemicals pass messages from one area to another or how they cause illnesses like cancer. Because anesthetics work with the body's chemicals, the future of anesthesiology is closely tied to the search for more information about the human body in general.

As researchers learn more about how drugs work in the body, they will create new drugs and find better ways to use current drugs more effectively. For example, researchers studying drugs that lower high blood pressure think that some blood pressure medication will be used with anesthetics in the future.

Anesthesiologists at the University of California at Los Angeles reported that one blood pressure drug, given before surgery, has cut by 40 to 50 percent the amount of gas and narcotics patients need during surgery. Anesthetists know that patients do better when they are not given too much medication. One day, this research with blood pressure drugs will help anesthetists safely reduce the amount of anesthetic they must give a patient during surgery.

Researchers are even finding easier ways to give anesthetic drugs to patients, especially children. Researchers are putting fentanyl, a popular painkiller for surgical pain, into lollipops. They are testing adults to see if the drug, taken in this form, can be effective. So far, the studies show the drugged lollipops produce sedation with few side effects. This method of giving drugs just before surgery will be helpful with children, who are too frightened or nervous to take a drug through an injection.

Scientists do not understand everything about how anesthetics work to block pain and induce sleep. Anesthesia research will focus on learning more about how these drugs work.

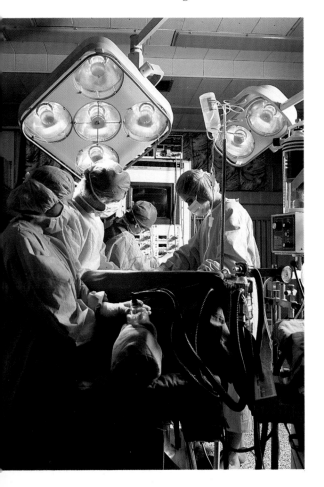

Eliminating Threats

As researchers learn more about drugs and about better ways to give them, some well-known drugs will become un-

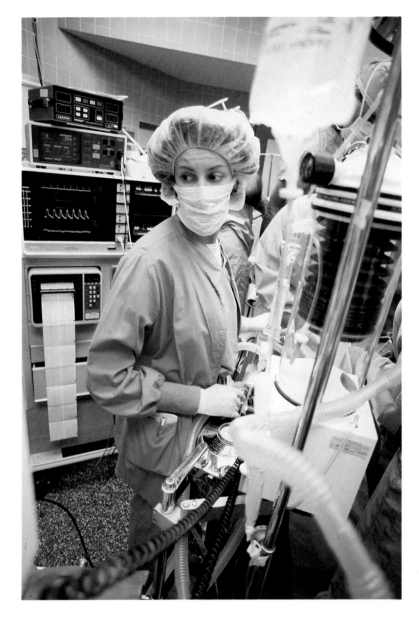

An anesthetist monitors a patient's vital signs. Because no anesthetic works perfectly, trained professionals must carefully monitor its use.

necessary and will be eliminated from operating rooms. By the end of this century, researchers predict, nitrous oxide will not be used during surgery.

Of the first three anesthetic gases—ether, chloroform, and nitrous oxide—only nitrous oxide continues to be used. Research now shows that this gas, once considered the safest, has dangers. It can be toxic to the heart, and it might cause cancer in people routinely exposed to it, like those who work in operating rooms.

Researchers have also learned that nitrous oxide reduces the amount of oxygen in a person's bloodstream. The gas's ability to deplete oxygen may have caused permanent brain and heart damage in countless patients before researchers knew enough to spot the damage and the gas's dangers. Because other anesthetics are safer than nitrous oxide, anesthetists no longer need to use it.

Nitrous oxide will not be the only discontinued anesthetic. Ongoing research with muscle relaxants will mean the end of succinylcholine, the synthetic replacement for curare. By the year 2000, anesthetists will use the extremely short-acting relaxants being tested in today's laboratories.

No matter how many drugs are replaced and no matter how much more people learn about anesthetic drugs, it is unlikely the future holds the discovery of the perfect anesthetic. Balanced anesthesia works so well because it uses the best qualities of several drugs to keep a patient safe and comfortable during surgery.

It is likely that researchers will concentrate on finding the best drug or drugs for inhalation, regional, local, and spinal anesthesia. They will look for the best painkillers, the best and safest sedatives, and the best muscle relaxants. They will be able to find these ideal drugs, however, only when they understand precisely how each of these drugs works in the body.

Computers in the Operating Room

The future of anesthesia also includes improving the equipment that delivers anesthetics into the body. Giving anesthesia is much more sophisticated than it was in the 1800s, when doctors put an ether-soaked rag under a patient's nose. Today's machines, however, may look as primitive as ether rags in comparison

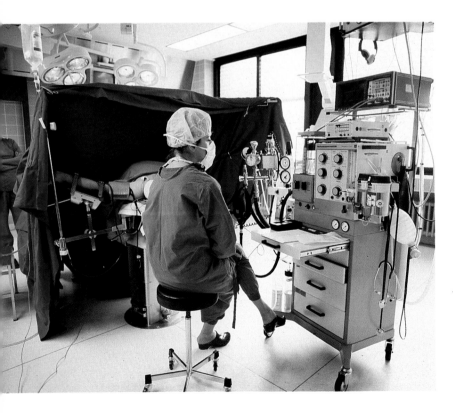

Computers help monitor a patient's body functions—such as heart rate and blood pressure—during surgery. In the future, the field of anesthetics will see even more sophisticated computers in the operating room.

with the equipment that will be used in the next decades.

Computer technology will dramatically change anesthesia equipment. Computers already monitor many of the body's functions during surgery. They keep track of the body's temperature, heart rate, and blood pressure. They already tell anesthetists how much oxygen patients have in their bloodstream and how much gas is being delivered into the lungs.

In the future, however, computers will also measure and record not only how much gas is in a patient's blood but also how much anesthetic is found in each part of the body and each organ. Doctors will be able to see where there is a buildup of metabolites, or toxins.

Machines of the Future

Anesthesia machines of the future may hold a variety of drugs—analgesics, sedatives, general and local anesthetics, and muscle relaxants—all at once. The dispenser for each type of anesthetic will be connected to a computer. Anesthetists will program the machines to deliver just the right combination of drugs to a patient.

By analyzing the data on the patient's heart rate, breathing rate, temperature, and blood pressure, these computers will be able to more closely monitor a patient's condition. They will be able to reverse, speed up, or stop a drug depending on how the patient's body is reacting, quickly giving the anesthetist complete information on which to base decisions about a patient's care.

The field of anesthesiology will continue to see the disappearance of old drugs, techniques, and equipment and

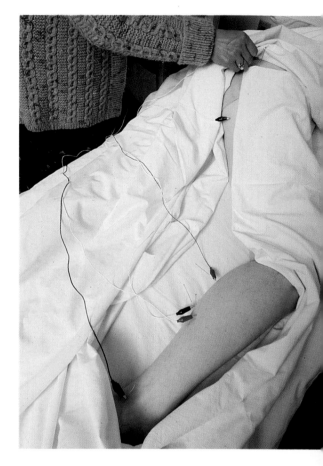

Acupuncture may ease or stop a patient's pain during surgery.

the appearance of new anesthetics and machines. The field may also see the return of old methods once thought of as too primitive or too uncertain.

Rethinking Acupuncture

Acupuncture and hypnosis may someday play a larger role in surgical anesthesia worldwide. In developing countries, where surgical equipment and anesthetic drugs are scarce, these methods offer a low-cost, nontechnical way to ease surgical pain.

In industrial countries like the

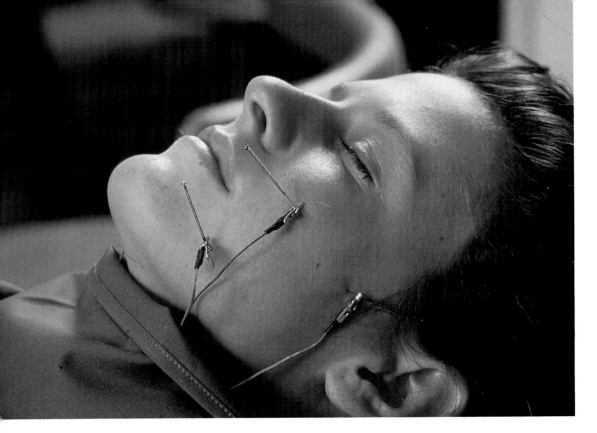

Fine needles are inserted in the face of a patient to deaden the sensation of pain. Although Western doctors do not fully understand how acupuncture works, they believe it blocks pain by disrupting electrical impulses sent through the body to the brain.

United States, people are looking for safe, healthy alternatives to drugs and technical medicine. Acupuncture and hypnosis may appeal to their wish to have better medicine without more chemicals.

Acupuncture has been used in China for centuries to ease and stop pain. But it has been used as a surgical anesthetic only since the 1960s, and many surgeries have been performed there using only acupuncture as the anesthetic.

This technique is rarely used in Western countries, where many patients and physicians do not understand or trust this procedure. Acupuncture was not even known in the United States until the 1970s, when the United States

and China renewed contact and exchanged cultural and scientific information.

Acupuncture is based on the belief that everything in life must be in balance, including health and illness. Chinese doctors believe the needles they stick into the body during acupuncture help restore the body's balance.

The acupuncturist inserts thin needles into one or several of the 365 acupuncture points along the body's electrical pathways. The healer rapidly twirls the needles while they are in the skin and then withdraws them. Some think that just like anesthetics, the needles ease or stop a patient's pain by disrupting the body's electrical impulses and keeping them from reaching the brain.

Before surgery, the doctor inserts the needles in the electrical pathways that control the area that will be cut. Sometimes, the patient is also stimulated by electrical current during the acupuncture session. After about twenty minutes of stimulation, the surgery begins.

Researchers admit that acupuncture seems to prove what doctors already know about the body—that seemingly unrelated parts of the body are somehow connected to each other. Doctors know, for example, that if you apply an ice pack to the lower chest, the blood vessels in the intestines will contract, even though the ice pack does not touch them. In other experiments, internal organs have been stimulated when specific spots along the spine are touched.

Many of those who study acupuncture think this method will be successful only in cultures where people believe in the mind's power to control the body. Many of the religions of the Far East, for example, stress the ability of the mind to overcome physical discomfort. These people may be more prepared mentally for acupuncture.

Hypnotic Trance

Hypnosis, the method of putting a person into a trance, also seems to work best as a painkiller in people who are willing to let their thoughts overpower their pain. Many modern doctors do not take hypnosis seriously. They often believe that the hypnotist or the patient fakes a trance or exaggerates the hypnotic effects.

A January 1991 article in the *American Journal of Clinical Hypnosis* predicts that in the next decade, researchers will pay more attention to how the mind and body work together during illness. Like acupuncture, hypnosis does not rely on expensive machinery or drugs. Hypnosis as a surgical anesthesia, says the author of the article, "would be ideal in the third world and in developing countries."

Hypnosis as a surgical anesthetic, in fact, was used in India, a third world country, ten months before William Morton gave his ether demonstration at Massachusetts General Hospital. British physician James Esdaile reported seventy-three painless surgical operations for amputations, tumors, eye operations, and tooth extractions. His report, however, was quickly overshadowed by the dramatic discovery of ether for painless surgery.

Does Hypnosis Work?

Doctors have known hypnosis works for some surgeries and with some people. What they do not know and what they will someday find out is what makes a particular person able to respond to hypnosis as a painkiller. With today's greater interest in self-healing, more people are willing to believe methods such as hypnosis and acupuncture can work, and they are more willing to support research into these techniques.

Hypnotherapists at the Johns Hopkins Medical School in Baltimore, Maryland, report that only one-third of patients are hypnotizable. Their figure is similar to figures in Chinese studies that reveal that only one-third of patients can benefit from acupuncture anesthesia. The figures from Johns Hopkins and China suggest that about one-third of all patients can respond to a psychological form of anesthesia. This type of anesthesia uses the brain as a powerful painkiller within the body.

Understanding Endorphins

Scientists want to know what happens in these patients' brains that enables them to block out pain. Do they share a common brain chemical or do they have more of some chemicals? Researchers are looking for answers to those questions.

Some researchers think these people are able to mentally release endorphins, chemicals that increase a person's ability to withstand pain. Endor-

(Top right) The pain-fighting abilities of endorphins make grueling, long-distance races bearable. (Below) A nurse treats an AIDS patient. Some researchers believe that anesthetics may someday play a role in the treatment of AIDS.

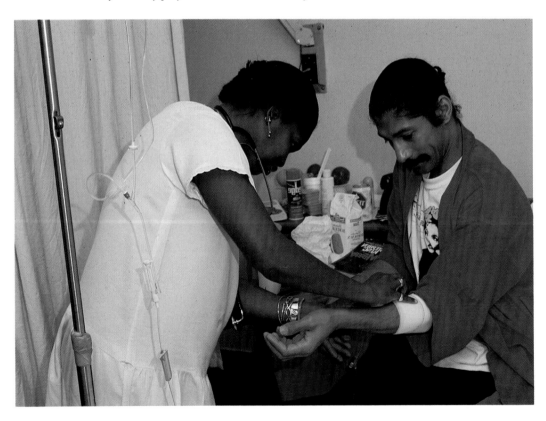

phins occur naturally in the body and are known to reduce pain. Researchers who study long-distance runners, for example, know that the runners' brains release endorphins as they run. Endorphins make it possible for marathon runners to endure physical pain during these grueling races. Researchers are looking for ways to use the body's natural pain-fighting abilities as anesthetics that can help patients block out pain in the future.

In the next decades, medical research may also find ways for anesthetics to stop the deadly effects of viruses and bacteria that invade the body. Medical researchers will continue to search for cures for diseases such as AIDS; Alzheimer's disease, a brain disorder that particularly affects older people; heart disease; and cancers of all kinds.

Researchers already know that anes-thetics disrupt nerve messages in healthy cells. They also know that metabolites from anesthetics can poison and damage cells. Can anesthetics or their toxic wastes disrupt the functioning of the AIDS virus? Can they stop the uncontrolled cell growth of cancers or alter the processes that cause Alzheimer's disease and heart trouble? Mark S. Scheller, an anesthesiologist at the University of California at San Diego reports that anesthetics that are toxic only to viruses or bacteria may play a role in the treatment and cure of these diseases.

Conquering Chronic Pain

Many researchers believe one of anesthesia's most significant future roles will be its conquest over all pain, not just surgical pain. "Our understanding of

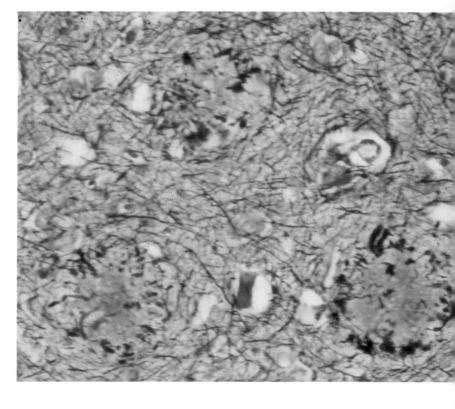

Researchers may someday be able to use anesthetics to cure Alzheimer's disease, a brain disorder that usually affects older people. Brain tissue from an Alzheimer's patient is pictured here.

the [cause], function, and treatment of pain has evolved very slowly over the last 50 years," Scheller says. Recent discoveries, however, about the role spinal pathways play in pain may be the key to understanding how pain works.

Given what researchers now know about pain, many believe the pain that comes from disease may be eliminated by the middle of the twenty-first century. Chronic, ongoing pain, they say, will be something people will only read about in history books. Chronic pain will not be something they personally experience

Today, however, chronic pain—the pain that comes with migraine headaches, arthritis, lower back pain, and pinched nerves—still invades the human body and still causes intense suffering. Physicians and researchers have been slow to look at ways of eliminating nonsurgical pain.

A director of a Canadian pain clinic says: "The tradition is that pain is a symptom of something else, so doctors look for the something else. They do not treat the pain." They have always assumed that if they cure the illness, they will cure the pain.

Some pain, however, is not caused by curable illness. People have had to learn

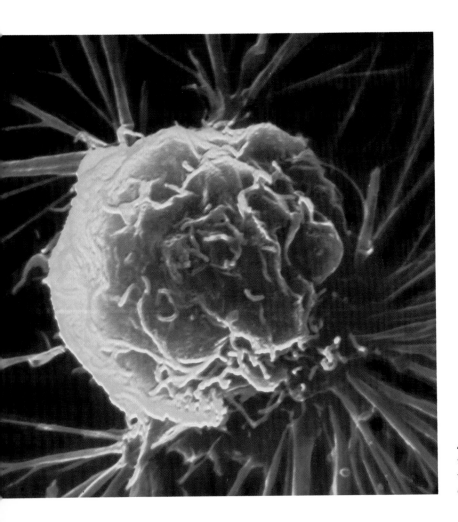

Someday anesthetics may be able to stop the uncontrolled cell growth of cancers.

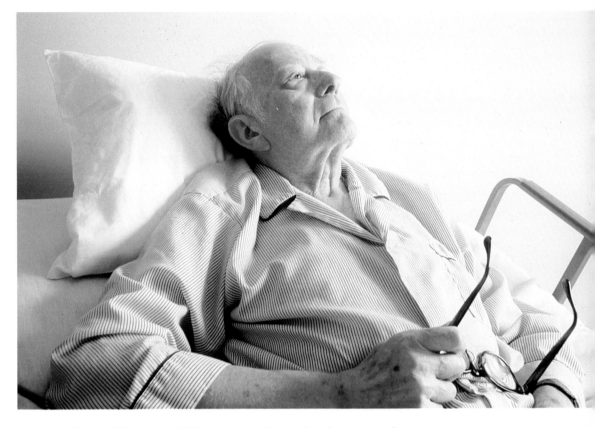

Many people live with chronic, debilitating pain. Researchers hope to someday use anesthesia to relieve all pain, not just surgical pain.

to live with the pain of crippling arthritis and rheumatism, for which there are no cures. Nerve damage from accidents or cancer brings excruciating pain.

Hopes for a Future Without Pain

Researchers are developing drugs to block pain impulses or to interfere with the body's pain signals. In France, researchers are using proteins in the body to strengthen the body's own painkilling chemicals. In England, researchers are studying hormones as possible pain-killers.

In Canada, test patients have had electrical stimulators planted in their brains to see if the impulses can stop pain in other parts of the body. Another Canadian doctor who was trained in Czechoslovakia is combining local anesthetics and acupuncture by injecting procaine into acupuncture spots. "The effect," he claims, "is instantaneous."

Researchers are trying to understand how pain works in the body so that they can learn how to control it. "The complete understanding and control of pain," says anesthesiologist Scheller, "is perhaps the greatest scientific challenge facing anesthesiologists." Pain, researchers hope, will be something future people never have to endure.

Glossary

acetylcholine: A chemical compound found where nerve endings and muscle fibers meet that sends nerve messages to the muscles so they can move.

acupuncture: An ancient Chinese system of healing in which pain is relieved by puncturing the skin in specific spots with fine needles.

alkaloid: Chemical substance found in plants that are often used to make drugs.

analgesia: Loss of the feeling of pain without loss of consciousness.

analgesic: A drug that relieves pain.

anesthesia: The loss of all feeling caused by a drug that blocks nerve impulses in all or part of the body.

anesthesiologist: A medical doctor who specializes in anesthesiology.

anesthetic: A drug that causes a loss of feeling in the body.

anesthetist: A doctor or registered nurse trained to give anesthesia.

barbiturate: Any of a large group of bitter-tasting drugs that cause sleep or anesthesia.

chloroform: A colorless, toxic, sweet-smelling liquid that gives off vapors that cause unconsciousness.

cocaine: A narcotic derived from the South American coca plant that works as a local anesthetic.

curare: A poison that causes rapid paralysis and death; made from compounds found in certain South American plants.

cyclopropane: A colorless, flammable gas used as an inhalation anesthetic.

endorphin: A chemical in the brain that helps ease pain.

endotracheal: Within the trachea, or windpipe.

epidural anesthesia: The method of injecting an anesthetic near the spinal cord.

epinephrine: A hormone that helps prolong the effects of local anesthetics.

ether: A strong-smelling liquid that easily gives off vapors that cause unconsciousness.

fluorine: A pale yellow, flammable, irritating, toxic gas used to make fluorinated anesthetics.

general anesthesia: The method of giving an inhaled gas or injected liquid to cause unconsciousness before surgery.

hypnosis: A condition similar to sleep in which a person easily responds to the suggestions or directions of another.

infiltration anesthesia: The method of making several shallow injections into or just under the skin to stop pain in the area surrounded by the injections.

inhalation anesthesia: The method of giving an anesthetic by having a person breathe a gaseous drug.

intravenous: Going into or through the veins.

local anesthesia: The method of injecting a drug to block pain in one area of the body without causing unconsciousness.

metabolites: A toxic-waste product that forms in the body when chemicals like anesthetics are broken down and changed into other substances.

narcotic: A drug that in small doses eases pain or brings a deep sleep but that in large amounts causes coma, convulsions, and even death.

nitrous oxide: A colorless gas that when inhaled can cause awkward movements and an inability to feel pain.

Novocain: A synthetic, local anesthetic created as a replacement for cocaine.

opium: A narcotic drug made from the opium poppy that brings a feeling of well-being and drowsiness and that in large amounts can cause death.

procaine: The first synthetic replacement for cocaine.

regional anesthesia: The method of injecting an anesthetic into a nerve center to block pain in a part of the body.

sedative: A drug that causes relaxation and sleepiness.

sodium Pentothal: A fast-acting barbiturate that can be used as a sedative or general anesthetic.

spinal anesthesia: The method of injecting an anesthetic into the fluid surrounding the spinal cord to cause a loss of feeling only in the lower half of the body.

succinylcholine: A synthetic version of curare.

synthetic: A substance made by combining various natural materials to imitate or replace something found in nature.

toxic: Poisonous.

For Further Reading

Rachel Baker, *Pioneer in the Use of Ether.* New York: Julian Messner, 1946.

M. Hashimoto, *Japanese Acupuncture.* New York: Liverright, 1966.

Larry Kettelkamp, *Hypnosis: The Wakeful Sleep.* New York: William Morrow, 1975.

Peggy L. Penney, *Surgery: From Stone Scalpel to Laser Beam.* New York: Thomas Nelson, 1977.

Victor Robinson, *Victory over Pain: A History of Anesthesia.* New York: Henry Schuman, 1946.

Irwin Shapiro, *The Gift of Magic Sleep: Early Experiments in Anesthesia.* New York: Coward, McCann & Geoghegan, 1979.

Philip Smith, *Arrows of Mercy.* Toronto: Doubleday Canada Limited, 1969.

Works Consulted

Paul G. Barash, Bruce F. Cullen, and Robert K. Stoelting, eds., *Clinical Anesthesia*. Philadelphia: Lippincott, 1989.

Frederick F. Cartwright, *The Development of Modern Surgery from 1830*. New York: Thomas Y. Crowell, 1968.

Barbara M. Duncum, *The Development of Inhalation Anesthesia: With Special References to the Years 1846-1900*. London: Oxford University Press, 1947.

Albert Faulconer Jr. and Thomas E. Keys, *Foundations of Anesthesiology. Vols. 1 and 2*. Springfield, IL: Charles C. Thomas, 1965.

Raymond Fink, "Leaves and Needles: The Introduction of Surgical Local Anesthesia," *Anesthesiology,* July 1985.

Rene Fulop-Miller, translated by Eden Paul and Cedar Paul, *Triumph over Pain*. New York: Literary Guild of America, 1938.

Howard W. Haggard, *Devils, Drugs, and Doctors: The Story of the Science of Healing from Medicine-Man to Doctor*. New York: Blue Ribbon Books, 1929.

Thomas E. Keys, *History of Surgical Anesthesia*. New York: Schuman's, 1945.

Richard B. Knapp, *The Gift of Surgery to Mankind: A History of Modern Anesthesiology*. Springfield, IL: Charles C. Thomas, 1983.

John Alfred Lee, *A Synopsis of Anaesthesia*. Bristol, England: John Wright & Sons, 1968.

David M. Little Jr., *Classical Anesthesia Files*. Park Ridge, IL: Wood Library-Museum of Anesthesiology, sponsored by the American Society of Anesthesiology, 1985.

Felix Mann, *Acupuncture: The Ancient Chinese Art of Healing and How It Works Scientifically*. New

York: Random House, 1971.

Howard Riley Raper, *Man Against Pain: The Epic of Anesthesia*. New York: Prentice-Hall, 1945.

J.E. Schmidt, *Medical Discoveries Who & When*. Springfield, IL: Charles E. Thomas, 1959.

David Shephard, "History of Anesthesia: John Snow and Research," *Canadian Journal of Anesthesia*, March 1989.

W.D.A. Smith, *Under the Influence: A History of Nitrous Oxide and Oxygen Anaesthesia*. London: Macmillan, 1982.

C. Ronald Stephen and David M. Little Jr., *Halothane (Fluothane)*. Baltimore: Williams & Wilkins, 1961.

K. Bryn Thomas, *The Development of Anaesthetic Apparatus*. London: Blackwell Scientific Publications, 1975.

Wynne R. Waugaman and Scot D. Foster, "New Advances in Anesthesia," *Nursing Clinics of North America*, June 1991.

Chris Wood, "Special Report: The Pain Barrier," *Maclean's*, February 27, 1989.

Ronald Woolmer, *The Conquest of Pain: Achievements of Modern Anaesthesia*. New York: Knopf, 1961.

Index

prolonging effects of, 42
used for painless dentistry, 25-27, 41-42
Novocain, 56-57

oxygen
  adding to cyclopropane, 60
  discovery of, 18
  effects of adding to nitrous oxide, 42

pain, chronic
  anesthesia's future role in stopping,
    83-85
painkillers
  used in ancient times, 12
Paracelsus, 15
Pasteur, Louis, 43
plants
  coca, 13, 45-46
  used by ancient people as anesthetics,
    12-13
Pravaz, Charles Gabriel, 48
Priestley, Joseph, 18
procaine, 56-57

Quincke, Heinrich I., 50-51

Richardson, Sir Benjamin Ward, 45

Scheele, Carl Wilhelm, 18
Schleich, Carl Ludwig, 53-54
Simpson, James
  experimented with chloroform, 35-36
  first to use ether for childbirth, 34
sleeping sponge, 14-15
Snow, John, 38
  chloroform inhaler of, 40
    illustrated, 39
  devised better ether inhalers, 40-41
Soubeiran, Eugene, 35
spinal anesthesia
  advantages of, 52-53

discovery of, 52
epidural procedure in, 50, 51
used during childbirth, 52-53
using cocaine in, 50
  disadvantages, 51-52
Stone Age
  anesthetics used during, 12-14
Suckling, Charles, 71-72
surgery
  ancient people's use of anesthetics
    during, 12-13
  chest, 64-65
  eye, cocaine as local anesthetic in, 47
  first painless, 10, 29-31
  germ-free, 43-44
  head, in ancient times, 12-13
  limit time for, 17-18
  using anesthetics during
    curare, 68-70
    ether, 23-25
surgical sponge, 14-15
sweet vitriol, 15-16

tooth extraction. *See* dentistry
trachea
  anesthetic gases flowing through, 63-
    65

unconsciousness
  John Snow's four stages of, 40

von Liebig, Justus, 35

Warren, John, 29-30
Waters, Ralph, 60, 63
Wells, Horace, 25-28, 31
Wood, Alexander, 48
Wren, Christopher, 59
Wright, Lewis, 68

About the Author

■■■

Judith C. Galas has been a reporter and free-lance writer for fifteen years and has reported from Montana, New York City, and London. She has a master's degree in journalism from the University of Kansas and makes her home in Lawrence, Kansas.

Picture Credits

Cover photo by FPG, Inc.
American Society of Anesthesiology, 66, 67 (top)
© Marvin Collins/Impact Visuals, 57 (top)
© Goivaux Communication/Phototake, 80
Historical Pictures/Stock Montage, 12,
　15(bottom), 17, 27 (bottom), 28 (top), 29, 34,
　67 (bottom)
© Ken Hoge/Phototake, 70, 77
© Ansell Horn/Impact Visuals, 53 (both), 82
　(bottom)
© Ed Kashi/Phototake, 79
© Scott Kilbourne/Uniphoto Picture Agency, 69
© Yoav Levy/Phototake, 56, 74, 85
Library of Congress, 13, 14, 15 (top), 16, 18
　(both), 19 (both) 20 (both), 21, 22, 23, 24
　(both), 25, 26, 27 (top), 28 (bottom), 30, 31,
　35, 36, 37, 38 (both), 40, 43 (both), 45, 47, 64
© Mauritius GMBH/Phototake, 75, 76, 78
National Library of Medicine, 41 (both), 42, 44,
　48, 49, 50, 52, 55, 57 (bottom), 61, 68
Northwind Picture Archives, 33
Phototake, 84
Photri, 46
© Martin M. Rotker/Phototake, 83
© Roger Sandler/Uniphoto Picture Agency, 82
　(top)
Renata Sobieraj, 58, 62, 65, 72
UPI/Bettmann, 73